RaisingBoys
With ADHD
Secrets for Parenting
Healthy, Happy Sons

RaisingBoys

With ADHD

Secrets for Parenting Healthy, Happy Sons

James W. Forgan, Ph.D., and Mary Anne Richey

PRUFROCK PRESS INC.
WACO, TEXAS

Library of Congress Cataloging-in-Publication Data

Forgan, James W.
 Raising boys with ADHD : secrets to parenting healthy, happy sons / by James W. Forgan and Mary Anne Richey.
    p. cm.
Includes bibliographical references.
ISBN 978-1-59363-862-7 (pbk.)
1. Attention-deficit hyperactivity disorder. 2. Attention-deficit-disordered children. 3. Child rearing. 4. Parent and child. I. Richey, Mary Anne, 1947- II. Title.
RJ506.H9F667 2012
618.92'8589--dc23
                        2011049297

Edited by Lacy Compton

Cover and layout design by Raquel Trevino

ISBN-13: 978-1-59363-862-7

At the time of this book's publication, all facts and figures cited are the most current available. All telephone numbers, addresses, and website URLs are accurate and active. All publications, organizations, websites, and other resources exist as described in the book, and all have been verified. The authors and Prufrock Press Inc. make no warranty or guarantee concerning the information and materials given out by organizations or content found at websites, and we are not responsible for any changes that occur after this book's publication. If you find an error, please contact Prufrock Press Inc.

Prufrock Press Inc.
P.O. Box 8813
Waco, TX 76714-8813
Phone: (800) 998-2208
Fax: (800) 240-0333
http://www.prufrock.com

Dedication

James dedicates this book to his number one son, Teddy, remembering the amazing times they've spent together riding ATVs, boating, and reading, as well as his wife, Peggy, for all of her love.

Mary Anne dedicates this book to her son and daughter, in celebration of the wonderful adults they have become, and to her tolerant and supportive husband.

124528

Table of Contents

Introduction

We know that behind every successful boy with ADHD is a tired parent. (Actually, we hope you are not alone. We hope you are surrounded by a strong supportive team, which could include a spouse, stepparents, grandparents, and even special friends and neighbors.) Raising a boy with ADHD can be exhausting, but we know you can do it. We know this because you wouldn't be reading this book if you didn't care deeply about your son. You will help guide him toward success in life. There is no *one* path to happiness and success, and it will be a journey influenced by parents, siblings, relatives, caregivers, teachers, and others. We've been down similar paths in our personal lives, and we also coach parents of boys with ADHD in our professional work. In this book, we've combined our success secrets to help guide you in raising your young man.

Your son with Attention Deficit/Hyperactivity Disorder (ADD/ADHD) is unique, special, and talented, and has his own set of strengths and skills. He has characteristics and abilities that you understand. You can nurture your son's qualities to help him grow into a successful man who will make you proud.

What Does Success for Boys With ADHD Look Like?

When we think about success, we don't view it in terms of "things." Being successful doesn't mean owning a fancy car or a huge house or having tons of money or an extraordinary career. Although these things can be nice and often project the image of success, they don't reflect internal success—the type of success you need to feel satisfied and fulfilled.

We've worked with too many families to know that what you see portrayed on the outside does not always mirror what's happening on the inside. One client told us, "My husband works so hard to support our lifestyle that he's filled with anxiety, takes medication, doesn't sleep well at night, and barely has time to spend with me or the kids." They drive expensive cars, send their kids to an exclusive private school, own a big house, and take luxurious vacations. Everything sure *seemed* OK to the casual observer, but happiness had eluded them.

In our opinion, success is about being happy with yourself and with what you have and believing that you make a difference in this world. This might come from making a difference in the life of your child or spouse, in your job, at your church, at a community center, or by helping others. Success for boys with ADHD is more about being capable of living independently, earning a living, and helping make our world a better place. As the country music song "Red Dirt Road" by Brooks and Dunn goes, "Happiness on Earth ain't just for high achievers." Sure, your son with ADHD *may* become a high achiever, but that alone isn't going to make him successful. It's your job as a parent to help your son identify his purpose, develop his talents, and learn how to get along with people. It's not a high-paying or cushy job, but it is *extremely* rewarding and, in our opinion, one of the most important jobs you'll ever do.

There is no doubt that raising a son is difficult, but raising a son with ADHD is even tougher. When you have a son with ADHD, you face issues that generally aren't on other parents' radar screens such as:

◊ years of telephone calls from his teachers,
◊ other parents' perceptions that you don't know how to discipline your son,
◊ being embarrassed by the impulsive things he says or does,
◊ the intensity of your son's emotional displays,
◊ his fragile self-esteem,
◊ his automatic negativity,
◊ discouragement (yours and his),
◊ relationship issues, and
◊ severe homework struggles.

That last one struck a chord, didn't it? Homework is usually an intense endeavor for boys with ADHD. The average boy may have some difficulty getting started on his homework, but with some gentle prompting, he starts and finishes within a reasonable time-frame. The boy with ADHD? He often has to conquer a personal battle just to get started, and it goes that way every night. His parents prompt, threaten, offer rewards (sometimes they look a little like bribes), and even sit next to their son for the entire time. Sound familiar? One mom told us that because of the continual battles she has with her son with ADHD over homework, she feels he doesn't even like her anymore. Another mother said, "I've battled him so long that I finally put him in aftercare at school so they could get him to do his homework."

Fortunately, there are professionals and resources to help you work through many of the parenting challenges of raising boys with ADHD. *You don't have to conquer everything on your own.* With some effort, you can find support groups with other parents of boys with ADHD, valuable books, and professionals such as counselors, psychologists, or medical doctors. Locating the right people to help you can take some energy, time on the phone, and research, but it *is* worth the effort. Not only will you feel less alone, but you'll also be making an investment in your son. As one wise mother of adult children told us, "You pay now or pay later." To us, it is much better to be proactive and provide assistance to ward off problems than to be reactive and face even larger problems. He may be too young or too immature to realize and verbalize it, but he'll thank you later.

If you do not have a professional to help guide you, don't worry. We are sharing some of our most valuable tips and strategies with you. At the end of each chapter, you will find points to consider and action steps you can take right away to help your child. Share these with your spouse or a family member so you'll have an ally in choosing the best strategies for supporting your son in school and at home. And once you've finished reading the book, we'll walk you step-by-step through creating a personalized Dynamic Action Plan. The beauty of your Dynamic Action Plan is that it will allow you and your son to build upon today's successes while following a blueprint for his promising future.

ADD Versus ADHD: What's the Difference?

Before you read too far in this book, we want to explain the ADHD and ADD terminology, because it can be confusing. Some professionals and parents use the acronyms ADD and ADHD interchangeably. Others use ADD to describe behaviors of forgetfulness, not paying attention, and distractibility; they apply the term ADHD to describe behaviors of hyperactivity and impulsivity. Within current professional literature, ADHD is considered the umbrella term that is used to describe both students with inattention as well as students with hyperactivity and impulsivity.

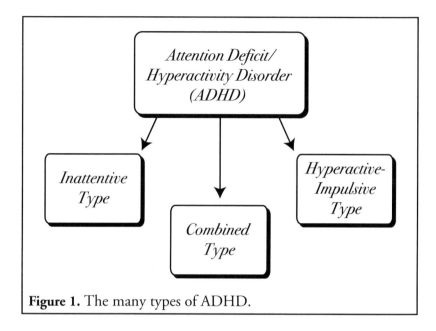

Figure 1. The many types of ADHD.

There is ADHD Predominantly Inattentive Type, which used to be called ADD. There is also ADHD Hyperactive-Impulsive, and that was called ADHD. There is also ADHD Combined Type, which is when a certain number of symptoms from both ADD and ADHD are met. In this book, we use ADHD as the general term that includes ADHD and ADD. The diagram in Figure 1 provides you with a visual of the many variations of ADHD.

Chapter 1

Coming to Terms: "My Son Has ADHD. Now What?"

You may not always recognize boys with ADHD, but believe us, they are *everywhere*. The American Psychiatric Association (2000) stated in its text revision of the fourth edition of the *Diagnostic and Statistical Manual of Mental Disorders* that "The prevalence of Attention-Deficit/ Hyperactivity Disorder has been estimated at 3%–7% in school age children" (p. 90). That's a lot of kids!

Furthermore, some organizations say up to 9.5% of the population has ADHD. According to the Centers for Disease Control and Prevention website (2011), 5.4 million children ages 5–17 have been diagnosed with ADHD by a healthcare professional. The CDC data showed that as of 2007, 2.7 million children in that age group were receiving medication for ADHD.

Assuming these numbers are accurate, a teacher can expect that at least 2 children in a class of 20 students will have ADHD. On a sports team of 12 players, there will be at least one with ADHD. In a church with a youth population of 100 children, at least 12 will have ADHD. How many kids live in your neighborhood? In addition to your own son, there are probably some boys with ADHD living around you. Boys (and girls) with ADHD are everywhere.

Did I Cause It?

Not intentionally. Nothing a parent *did* causes ADHD, but in many cases, a parent's genetics probably contribute.

Because he doesn't look physically different, it might be difficult to accept that your son has a problem. This can be especially true for fathers. Often in a dad's eyes, his boy is just being a boy. He is *supposed* to be active and run around, climb things, ask a million questions, and argue. We often hear from dads, "It's the same thing I did as a kid." Pause on that thought. This is a key point because most professionals consider ADHD to be a neurobiological condition that is heavily rooted in genetics. When Jim's son was diagnosed, the psychologist asked Jim if he thought he had ADHD or if it was suspected in his wife's family tree. In fact, for their family, ADHD had been suspected but had never been officially diagnosed.

When a child is diagnosed with ADHD, parents often comment to us that their son is a lot like they were as a child. It doesn't help one bit to cast blame on yourself or your spouse and wonder who your son "got it" from. If you do suspect a genetic link, try instead to find some sympathy and compassion for what your son is facing.

Many parents feel guilt-ridden because they believe their actions may be responsible for their son's ADHD. Parents may even start to second-guess themselves by making negative assumptions. Parents have told us:

◇ "I should have breast-fed him instead of using the bottle."
◇ "I should have played with him more."

◇ "I shouldn't have let him watch so much television or play so many video games."

◇ "Letting the nanny watch him while I worked was a mistake."

◇ "If I had not put him in that preschool with that mean teacher, then this would not have happened."

◇ "If only his dad had taken more interest in him as a youngster."

◇ "I shouldn't have fought with him all the time."

It is important for you to remember that your parenting style and the decisions you've made usually are not your son's main issues. Being a more skilled parent will not make ADHD go away. Poor parenting does not *cause* ADHD (but as we'll see later in the book, it certainly can aggravate the situation). Can we, as parents, improve the way we deal with our sons with ADHD? Absolutely, and we'll spend a good bit of this book sharing ways to help you do just that.

When parents come to us for professional advice and help, we reassure them that their parenting skills did not cause their son's ADHD. Even though most parents may realize this, they are still relieved to hear it from a professional. Mary L., a parent of a 9-year-old son with ADHD, expressed this: "After all these years, I was relieved. I'm sure parents in my neighborhood thought John's behavior was my fault, but it's not. It's his ADHD that causes him to become so emotional." Another parent, Amy S., explained it this way: "It's like a chip was missing in his brain. When Mark was young and he wanted people to go home, he would just yell, 'Make them go home!' I used to get so embarrassed."

Taking Charge of ADHD

We often advise parents not to worry so much about the label but to focus on proactive steps they can take to help their son. To raise a successful son with ADHD, you must start doing things differently from the day you find out your son has ADHD.

Recognize That ADHD Is a Disability

Even though your son may look fine on the outside, his mind is wired very differently. Taking a "disability perspective" provides understanding. You are taking a great step by reading this book and teaching yourself more about ADHD. Increasing your knowledge about ADHD is key to raising a successful son.

Try to Become More Understanding and Patient

That doesn't mean you will let your son "get away with things," but you will need to learn to respond differently. When Jim gets upset or frustrated with his son, he tends to point his index finger at Teddy and shake it up and down as he scolds him. Jim became so frustrated at himself that he was determined to stop this automatic response. One day he decided to write the letters "u" and "p" on the edge of his finger. When he got upset and pointed his finger at Teddy, Jim got an automatic visual reminder to have understanding and patience. This simple strategy worked!

Locate Support Personnel

Begin to locate different support personnel such as educators, counselors, and doctors who can serve as resources throughout the years. Part of raising a successful son with ADHD is recognizing that it's very tough to try to do alone. If your son is going to be successful, at the very minimum you must have his teachers' support.

Prepare for the Long Haul

Realize that you and your son are going to have really good periods and really rough patches and that meaningful change will occur over time. Remember that maturation helps most boys with ADHD, and as they move from the preschool to upper elementary years, the tantrums and tears tend to decrease.

ADHD Is Real

At times you still may wonder, or have to convince a skeptical family member, whether or not ADHD is a fad or made-up disorder. Rest assured, ADHD is not a diagnosis contrived by parents or professionals looking for an excuse for a child's behavior.

As a parent, the key to explaining ADHD to others is to first thoroughly understand it yourself. Professionals and laypeople use different words to explain ADHD. In his book, *Dr. Larry Silver's Advice to Parents on ADHD*, Dr. Larry Silver (1999) described ADHD as a "neurologically based disorder" (p. 3). The National Dissemination Center for Children with Disabilities (2010) noted that "ADHD is a condition that can make it hard for a person to sit still, control behavior, and pay attention" (para. 4). The core symptoms of ADHD are developmentally inappropriate levels of inattention, hyperactivity, and impulsivity. In line with this, the National Resource Center on ADHD (2008) defined ADHD as "a condition affecting children and adults that is characterized by problems with attention, impulsivity, and over activity" (para. 1).

Russell Barkley, an eminent researcher in the field of ADHD, added that

> Most recent theories of ADHD have viewed behavioral inhibition as central to the disorder, while also suggesting that deficits in executive function and self-regulation are likely to account for part or all of the inattentive symptoms associated with the disorder. (p. 39)

These definitions have the following in common: ADHD is highly disruptive, involves too much energy or being too distracted, and is neurologically based. The behaviors must occur to a degree that is highly atypical of children the same age and must interfere with academic or social progress. Finally, the behaviors must occur across multiple settings.

Nor is ADHD unique to the postmodern era. As early as 1845, a German physician wrote a poem about "Fidgety Philip," a boy who can't sit still at dinner and accidentally knocks all of the food onto the floor, to his parents' great displeasure. This is one of the earliest records of symptoms consistent with what we now call ADHD.

A great deal of research in the 1940s and 1950s focused on disorders of the brain. Scientists described ADHD-like behavior with terms such as "minimal brain dysfunction" or "hyperkinetic impulse disorder." In 1987, the third edition of the *Diagnostic and Statistical Manual of Mental Disorders* recognized the disorder as Attention Deficit Hyperactivity Disorder. Thus, the notion that ADHD is a disorder made up in the 1990s is a myth because behaviors related to ADHD have been recorded for more than 100 years.

Many other myths about ADHD still exist (see Table 1). Are there any you still believe?

Table 1

Myths and Facts About ADHD

Myth	Fact
Poor parenting causes ADHD.	ADHD is neurological and often genetic.
If you have one child with ADHD, all of your children will have it.	Not all children in the same family have ADHD.
ADHD is not a disability.	ADHD is a recognized disability in the Americans with Disabilities Act (ADA) and the Individuals with Disabilities Education Act (IDEA).
Medication is the only treatment for ADHD.	Medication is only one treatment option.
Schoolteachers want active boys on medication.	Schoolteachers want their students to give their best effort.
If a boy is hyper, then he has ADHD.	Boys who are hyper do not always have ADHD. Other things, such as anxiety, can cause hyperactive types of behaviors.
A boy who is quiet and likes to read cannot have ADHD.	Some boys who have the inattentive type of ADHD are quiet and like to read.
Schools do not know how to teach boys with ADHD.	Schools are becoming more knowledgeable and must provide appropriate accommodations to boys with ADHD.
Only a psychiatrist can diagnose ADHD.	Pediatricians, psychologists, neurologists, psychiatrists, and other mental health and medical personnel can all diagnose ADHD.
Psychologists prescribe medication.	Only medical doctors such as pediatricians, neurologists, and psychiatrists and nurse practitioners can prescribe medication.
An equal number of boys and girls are diagnosed with ADHD.	More boys than girls are diagnosed with ADHD.
Boys with ADHD want to behave badly.	Boys with ADHD are not able to behave consistently, independently, or predictably.
ADHD is a societal fad and will go away.	ADHD has been recognized since the mid-1800s but has been called by different names.
ADHD and ADD are the same thing.	ADHD is an umbrella term that is used in the DSM-IV criteria in place of ADD, a term found in previous DSM editions. ADD was renamed in 1994 by the American Psychiatric Association (APA).

ADHD Properly Diagnosed

Have you ever asked yourself, "Why seek a professional diagnosis? Why not just begin a homeopathic or behavioral treatment?" One dad, a prospective client of Jim's, called and asked abruptly, "Why should I drop a grand with you to diagnose my son when I can just start counseling?" Jim explained that a thorough evaluation and proper diagnosis help determine the most appropriate treatment.

Let's face it: You can build a house without a set of plans. It may take a lot longer, cost a lot more, and have hidden problems, but it can be done. Likewise, do you think a smart general enters a war without a battle plan? Absolutely not. So why start treating your son for something you suspect but haven't confirmed?

The diagnosis serves multiple purposes. First, it may provide parents with a sense of understanding, which is often accompanied by relief. Parents may be relieved to know their child really does have something fundamentally different about his mind. The diagnosis also can help parents shift their mindset about their child.

Second, the diagnosis may provide you and your son with access to school services. Most public and private schools require a professional diagnosis or an evaluation to provide any formal accommodations. Accommodations are adjustments such as extra time to complete tests or homework, seating near the front of the class, or frequent breaks. Furthermore, as boys with ADHD prepare to take college entrance exams, a diagnosis and a complete evaluation report by a qualified individual are required to receive accommodations.

Third, the diagnosis allows you, if you desire, the option of trying medication. Not all parents want to try prescribed medication with their child. If you decide to do so, you must have a proper diagnosis before obtaining a prescription. Some medical doctors will write a prescription based only on their own examination of the boy without a psychologist's written report. We recommend both a psychological and medical evaluation of your child before pursuing medical treatment. Both the psychologist and the pediatrician are important members of your son's team. One of the secrets to success is that the stronger the team, the more thorough and accurate the diagnosis.

You must educate yourself about ADHD so that you can advocate for your child. After all, if you don't advocate for your son, who will? He does not want to go to school and fail, play sports and get yelled at by the coach, or be excluded from friends' social activities because he says inappropriate things at the wrong time. Your son needs you to be strong, to be his voice when he is weak, and to encourage others to treat him fairly. Without you, your son can be at a great disadvantage in school, sports, friendships, gatherings, and life. You are a source of encouragement and support that is invaluable. Even though you will become discouraged at times, frustrated by his behavior, and embarrassed by things he does, you love your son—and your son loves you. Your hard work will pay off and you'll feel rewarded. So let's move on and discuss how you can determine if your son's behavior is typical or atypical.

Typical Versus Atypical Behavior

We're often asked, "How do you determine if this is normal boy behavior or behavior that is unusual?" You can probably arrive at an answer on your own, but you need to consider these three questions to know if your son's behavior is unusual:

◇ How frequently does the disruptive behavior occur?
◇ How long do your son's disruptive behaviors last?
◇ How intense is your son's behavior during this time?

Think about how frequently your son's disruptive behaviors occur. Once an hour? Once a day? Once per week? It is unusual for a child to get into trouble on a daily basis. We talked to one mom who felt like she had to keep her 7-year-old away from the other neighborhood boys because every time her son went out to play, he came home crying. He had an explosive temper and yelled at the other boys when he got mad but couldn't handle it when the neighborhood kids yelled back, and he'd run home in tears. This was unusual behavior because it happened so consistently.

Consider the parent with several sons who all have similar behavior patterns. They may think their children are behaving typically because their reference group of boys may be their only comparison. Thus, parents may think that everything is fine until their sons go to school. Once a young boy enters the school system, the parents are surprised to learn that their son's behavior is considered problematic.

Or what about the preschool boy who urinates on a tree during recess? Think about the middle school boy who taunts other children. Are these typical boy behaviors or alarming actions? In both situations, parents and teachers have to consider the context of the behaviors. The boy who urinated on the tree may have done this on occasion when there was an emergency and a bathroom was too far away. Maybe he and Daddy go on trees when hunting, fishing, or camping, and he genuinely thought it was OK in the schoolyard as well. The middle school student may live in a neighborhood or home environment where taunting is considered part of survival and standing up for himself. Remember, in order for a behavior to fall under the ADHD umbrella, it must interfere with the boy's functioning and occur so frequency that it is considered problematic.

The second question was, "How long do your son's disruptive behaviors last?" Are the behaviors like a brief passing rain shower or long and drawn-out? Think about a boy who is upset because he wants to play video games but has to do his homework. Depending on their age, most boys become upset and huff and puff around, and yet recover within an age-appropriate amount of time. Time tends to heal things with most boys. Take the same situation for the boy with ADHD. You give him a 5-minute warning to prepare him for the change. Then you give a 2-minute warning that video game time is almost finished. Still, he just can't seem to stop playing or being upset that game time is over. It takes the boy with ADHD much longer to redirect his focus from one fixation toward something else, particularly something he perceives as unpleasant (like homework). At home and school, boys with ADHD are constantly required to shift their thoughts. Boys who have difficulty with cognitive flexibility often dislike unexpected changes in routine.

The third question we asked you to consider was, "How intense is your son's behavior during this time?" If your son's temper tantrum goes on for hours and is so severe that no one wants to (or is able to) get near him, the intensity would be considered severe. When parents, teachers, and school staff meet to discuss the boy's disruptive behavior in relation to frequency, duration, and intensity, parents' eyes may be opened to recognize that a potential problem exists.

Other groups of parents suspect, from an early age, that their son is having behaviors related to inattention or hyperactivity. These parents either may have other children without behavior difficulties or may be alert to the differences they see by observing friends' children in play groups, sports, or church activities. They realize their child may be more emotional or active than other children. These parents often seek help on their own.

Eventually both groups of parents reach a point when they understand their child may have behaviors related to ADHD. At this point they begin to learn more about what ADHD means. For example, Joan's son was only 4 years old but had been kicked out of three preschools for biting, kicking, hitting, and disruptive behavior. The fourth school worked with her until Sam entered a public kindergarten, where within the first month he was in trouble for his behavior in afterschool care. The family came to see Jim when Sam's parents were told he could not return to afterschool care once the month ended. Even the classroom teacher had difficulty managing Sam. Clearly, the parent was not surprised that Sam's behavior went beyond typical boy behavior.

Jim completed a comprehensive evaluation and used tools to assess Sam's memory, attention, auditory and visual processing, and academics. He talked to Sam's parents and teacher. They also completed rating scales. At the end of the evaluation process, Jim sat down with Sam's parents and explained how their son met the criteria for ADHD and not other disorders that could have caused the behavior problems. Together, they set up an action plan so the parents knew exactly what to do. This was a better option for everyone—Sam, his family, his teacher, and his school—than taking a "wait-and-see" approach.

How Long Does ADHD Last?

Most researchers agree that ADHD lasts a lifetime. "Numerous longitudinal studies now support the conclusion that ADHD is a relatively chronic disorder affecting many domains of major life activities from childhood through adolescence and into adulthood" (Barkley, 2006, p. 40). The impact of ADHD on adults will likely become as widely studied as its impact on children.

Some encouraging news is that puberty or maturation changes types of ADHD behaviors for some boys. According to Silver (1999), "About 40–50 percent of children with ADHD will improve or no longer have ADHD after puberty" (p. 18).

Mary Anne's son loved playing school sports and became active in student government and a number of clubs in middle school and high school. His activity level remained high throughout puberty but was channeled in many different directions and became a definite positive for him. What did change was his knowledge about his strengths and limitations and his ability to work around his shortcomings. He didn't engage in risk-taking behavior more than the average teenage boy and was not sensation-seeking. All in all, his teenage years were very rewarding.

Your son's experience with ADHD during and after puberty will be unique. Many of our clients have noticed decreases in their son's impulsive behavior after puberty. Sheila S. explained her observations: "After he hit the ninth grade, Felix did not seem as hyperactive and could actually remain seated throughout a whole church service and even made it through a wedding ceremony." Other parents say their son still shows excessive movement but is able to channel the energy into appropriate behaviors. One mom told us, "He still moves a lot, but now when he sits it's his leg moving up and down, as compared to his entire body."

The important perspective is to have hope that your son's ADHD may decrease during puberty but to recognize that it may not. Regardless of the outcome, stand ready to give your son the support he needs.

Is ADHD a Gift?

The answer to this question is no. *And* yes.

There will be countless times when your son's ADHD seems far more like a burden than a gift. Many people you encounter tend to point out the negatives about ADHD. You'll hear comments like these:

◊　"He talks too much."

◊　"He won't sit still."

◊　"He annoys other students around him."

◊　"He causes disruption in my class."

◊　"He won't listen."

◊　"He makes inappropriate comments."

The list goes on and on, and you can almost certainly add to it. We've found that most kids with ADHD hear many more negative than positive comments.

Especially when your son with ADHD is in preschool and early elementary school, he will likely have difficulty conforming to school rules, expectations, and behavior. He won't consider his ADHD a gift, and you probably won't either. Most elementary schools are not set up to accommodate active boys. When our sons were in kindergarten, they were expected to sit on the carpet in front of the teacher and listen to her read a book. This was difficult for Teddy because his body needed to move. He preferred to shift around on the carpet, lay down, then get up again, often inadvertently touching his neighbor. His teacher found this bothersome; not only did he get in trouble, but he was moved to the back of the carpet or made to sit at his desk. In the elementary classroom, his ADHD was not a gift.

So when *can* ADHD become a blessing? When your son's natural talents are harnessed in the right direction, ADHD can be a gift at any age. For many boys it becomes a gift in the outdoors; while building; when participating in sports, extracurricular activities, art, music, or academic subjects that interest him; or when he's interacting with people. Many argue that ADHD is a gift because individuals with ADHD often have talents that others lack and a high-energy level that enables them to accomplish many things.

You understand your son with ADHD best, so think about his talents. What are they? Your insight will help you identify his strengths. Ask yourself these types of questions:

◊   What comes naturally to my son?
◊   What does he enjoy spending time doing?
◊   If asked, what would family or friends identify as his talents?
◊   What type of career do I picture for my son?

Our sons are usually described as being social, exciting, funny, loving, risk-taking, and energetic. These positive qualities should not be overlooked and can become huge assets when they are adults. Jim once attended a seminar by Dr. John C. Maxwell, an international leadership expert, who advised parents not to focus on weaknesses but to find, build, and nurture their children's strengths. Buy books on topics your son enjoys, talk with experts, attend seminars, and take field trips. Dr. Maxwell stressed that your child's strengths will carry him through life. If your child is a C student in reading, perhaps you should be OK with that. Instead of spending hours and hours working with tutors, DVDs, and worksheets in an attempt to mold him into an A-level reader, spend time building on his strengths instead. If you like this notion, you may enjoy Dr. Maxwell's 2007 book, *Talent Is Never Enough*.

Mary Anne's son demonstrated strengths in leadership and athletics. He had high energy, a quality that many other teens enjoy. He was able to see the big picture and organize people toward a common goal, something he currently does in his career of biomedical engineering. To get to that point, Mary Anne and her husband worked with him to find areas that interested him. When he signed up for a sport or activity, he knew he couldn't quit but didn't have to sign up again if it wasn't something he wanted to pursue. You will spend time and energy in helping a boy with ADHD develop his interests and strengths. But that time and energy pays big dividends in self-esteem, helps him form a basis for friendships, and provides him with constructive ways to spend his time.

Boys with ADHD often have strengths in many areas. Your son has more strengths than you and he have probably identified. Look at the list in Figure 2 and check off all of the areas of strength that apply to your son.

Now that you've identified some of your son's strengths, build upon them. Consider making a list of his talents and special qualities and posting it where you both can be reminded of them. Provide various opportunities for your son to develop these strengths as well as discover new hidden talents. Your son has gifts that can take

❏ creative	❏ artistic	❏ outdoorsy
❏ intuitive	❏ exuberant	❏ sensitive
❏ emotionally expressive	❏ funny	❏ flexible
❏ kind	❏ considerate	❏ thoughtful
❏ energetic	❏ humorous	❏ imaginative
❏ smart	❏ attractive	❏ curious
❏ athletic	❏ friendly	❏ visual
❏ likes building	❏ likes designing	❏ musical
❏ spontaneous	❏ effective in problem solving	❏ can be a leader
❏ works quickly	❏ processes information quickly	❏ sees solutions quickly

Figure 2. Strengths of boys with ADHD.

him far and help him have a happy and satisfying adult life. It's our job as parents of boys with ADHD to nurture those talents.

Explaining ADHD to Others

If your son has ADHD, should you tell other people? Has your son's behavior embarrassed you? Do you worry about people judging your parenting skills and your son? Are you concerned with your child having a label? These are some of the issues parents ask us about, and they are questions that don't always have easy answers.

If your son has ADHD, then chances are excellent that you have been embarrassed by his behavior at one point or another. Sometimes parents wish they could hide in a shell. One mother of a 9-year-old boy told us, "I got a call from the school principal. She said my son was saying inappropriate sexual things during car line.

I don't have a clue where he heard them because we never use such talk around him."

Even Jim has found himself embarrassed when his son Teddy's behavior was less than perfect. He remembers picking Teddy up from Sunday school—a place you really want your child to be at his best—and being faced with reports of the various ways Teddy had misbehaved. In fact, sometimes Jim and his wife took turns picking Teddy up, just so one of them could be spared the discomfort of hearing the rundown if something had gone wrong that particular week.

As a parent of a son with ADHD, you have to develop what some people call a "thick skin," because others may judge *you* based on *your son's* behavior. Most boys with ADHD are active, energetic, and enthusiastic children who love excitement. They would much rather play with toys they can smash, crash, and trash in ways that seem to defy logic. Parents who only have girls don't seem to understand this and often become annoyed by this type of play.

Years later, Jim can finally laugh when he remembers the Christmas when 6-year-old airplane-crazy Teddy got three Playmobil toy sets. The sets were too advanced for Teddy to build alone, so Jim spent 3 hours building an airport and airplanes, adhering the tiny stickers, and arranging the furniture and accessories. Teddy couldn't wait to fly his planes. "What I didn't expect," Jim recalls,

> was that instead of landing the airplane next to the airport, Teddy landed it *in* the airport with a huge crash and smashed it to pieces! Three hours of building and perfecting the set and it was destroyed in seconds. That wouldn't have been so bad, but then he flew his airplane right into his sister's brand-new Playmobil grocery store and just about annihilated it. Teddy's mom stared in disbelief. She grew up without brothers and didn't always get his behavior.

> I explained that boys, especially boys with ADHD,
> prefer this type of smash-and-crash play.

The sooner you can quickly explain ADHD to others, the sooner you will help pave your son's road to success. If you're comfortable, you can have a heart-to-heart conversation about your son's ADHD, but sometimes those kinds of talks just aren't possible. Figure 3 is a sample letter you might use to explain your son's diagnosis to loved ones. Rewrite it, insert your son's name, and customize it so it has the right feel for the recipient and for your situation.

Depending on your family dynamic, you might choose to discuss your son's diagnosis in person with his siblings, share it with them in a letter, or some combination of the two. Figure 4 is an example of how you can explain ADHD to siblings.

Figure 5 is a letter Jim gave to Teddy's first-grade teacher before the school year started. It highlighted his strengths and potential areas of weakness and also offered suggestions of strategies that had proven to be effective. Each year through elementary school, the Forgans wrote a letter like this. Additionally, they met with the teacher either before the first day of school or within the first week of school.

Explaining ADHD to Your Son

You need to tell your son about his ADHD. You want him to understand ADHD, but you don't want him to use it as a crutch or an excuse for failing to behave or achieve his potential.

The Younger Child

We believe you can explain ADHD to elementary-aged children. You may find it easier to explain by reading a children's book

Dear _____ ,

   This isn't an easy letter to write, but it is an important one—and you're a very important person in (insert son's name)'s life. Not long ago I took _____ for a series of tests and activities to find out how he learns best, and whether there were any areas of concern. The psychologist gathered input from me, from _____'s teacher, and from observing _____. Based on the evaluation results and the input from everyone, he/she concluded that _____ has Attention Deficit/Hyperactivity Disorder or ADHD.

   There are a lot of myths about ADHD, so I wanted to make sure you have good, solid information about it. ADHD is a medical condition and one of the most well-researched childhood disorders. It is not a fad or an excuse for bad behavior or lack of motivation. His brain is wired very differently from most other children's, which means that while he's a bright boy, he'll have to work much harder than others his age. Learning does not always come easily to him.

   Many of our daily struggles are related to his ADHD. _____'s ADHD behaviors occur in school, at home, and with friends. This is why life is tough for him. He never gets a break from having ADHD. We've learned that _____'s brain is actually understimulated in the areas that maintain focus, deal with frustration, and apply what he knows consistently, predictably, and independently. This is why _____ can focus on something he really likes but has such a hard time focusing on things that don't interest him. It also explains why he can be so inconsistent in his behavior. It's all related to ADHD.

   We are now using strategies at school and at home to try to minimize the effects of _____'s ADHD to help him and the whole family. It's a long road ahead and we all need your support along the way. There will be ups and downs as we teach _____ how to deal with ADHD. Please try to be as understanding and patient with _____ as you can. That's what I'm doing, and each day is a work in progress.

   I have a lot more I can share, and I hope we can talk about _____ more soon.

Figure 3. Letter to family member.

about ADHD to your son. Reading books helps your son identify with the book's character and realize that he is not alone with his ADHD. A book also becomes a nonthreatening way for you to have a simple conversation about school and behavior. Because children's books go in and out of print, you'll need to check with

Dear (<u>insert sibling's name</u>),

I want to share something very important with you. You know that (<u>insert brother's name</u>) has a hard time when he gets frustrated or upset. You've seen him get mad and say mean things or even hit you. He doesn't want to behave that way, but his mind works differently. He knows what he should do but can't always make the right choices. He reacts before he thinks things through.

I took _____ to a doctor who said he has Attention Deficit/Hyperactivity Disorder or ADHD. This is something he was born with, and no one person or thing caused it. Lots of people have ADHD, even famous people. Some people even think Albert Einstein may have had ADHD. It's something that _____ is learning to deal with, and so are we. We are working with his teacher at school to make sure he does well there.

At home we're going to be trying some things to help _____ and everyone get along together. It's going to take a lot of work, and there are still going to be blow-ups along the way, but we're on the right track. You can help by being patient with _____ and guiding him to make right choices. I'm always here for any questions you have, and if you can't think of any now, you can always ask me later.

Love,
Mom/Dad

Figure 4. Letter to sibling.

your local library or search online for recent books. These are a few books currently available to explain ADHD to a younger boy:

◊ *Putting on the Brakes: Understanding and Taking Control of Your ADD or ADHD* (Patricia O. Quinn & Judith M. Stern)

◊ *Cory Stories: A Kid's Book About Living With ADHD* (Jeanne Kraus)

◊ *Otto Learns About His Medicine: A Story About Medication for Children With ADHD* (Matthew R. Galvin)

◊ *Why Can't Jimmy Sit Still?: Helping Children Understand ADHD* (Sandra L. Tunis)

Dear (insert teacher's name),

Teddy is outgoing and athletic. He is a gifted athlete and excels in most physical sports. This summer he learned to water-ski and got up on his third try. He loves insects and is the expert lizard catcher in our neighborhood. He also knows a lot about fishing. He really enjoys hands-on projects and kinesthetic learning.

Teddy learns and remembers best when he has the opportunity to learn through multiple modes such as hearing, seeing, and moving. He has really taken to reading using the multisensory approach based on Orton-Gillingham principles. This summer Teddy worked with a tutor who uses the Wilson Reading System, and he is good at "tapping" out sounds. Ask him to tap out a word for you like "hot" or "tub." Because of his ADHD, Teddy works best when he can take short breaks during and between assignments. It may be helpful to have him repeat the instructions back to you (without embarrassing him, as he is very sensitive to criticism).

Teddy has an older sister, and they get along very well. We are glad Teddy is off to a great start in your class.

Sincerely,
Jim and Peggy Forgan

Figure 5. Letter to school/teacher.

The 'Tween or Teen

If your middle school or teenage son has just been diagnosed with ADHD, you'll handle it a bit differently. Ideally, the person who officially diagnosed your son will give him an age-appropriate explanation of his ADHD. This is a brief way we explain it to our teenage clients:

> Marlon, the testing you completed with me showed that you have quite a few strengths, and some of them include (*fill in the blank with his strengths*). The testing also showed there are some things that are much harder for you, compared with other boys your age. For example, you mentioned that it is difficult for you to (*fill in the blank: complete*

your homework, turn in your homework, stay seated for a length of time, remain organized, study for tests, etc.). This difficulty is related to Attention Deficit/ Hyperactivity Disorder or ADHD. Have you heard of ADHD? The testing results confirmed that you have ADHD. What this means is that you are smart, outgoing, creative, and hardworking, but because of the way your mind is wired, you have difficulty with (*fill in the blank*). This difficulty is not going to stop you from being successful in school; it won't stop you from going to college or technical school or having a good career. You can be successful, but you are going to have to work harder than many boys. It also means that you may need more support like having a counselor, coach, or person to help guide you. You and your family may consider trying medication or supplements to help you. The important thing for you to remember is that you can't use your ADHD as an excuse not to do well in school. As I already said, you can be successful, but it takes hard work. There are many successful men with ADHD such as Michael Phelps, Ty Pennington, Jim Carrey, and lots of others. What questions do you have?

If the professional you worked with did not explain ADHD to your son, you can provide the explanation, and books can fill in the gaps. Here are resources you can share with your older son:

◊ *The ADHD Workbook for Teens: Activities to Help You Gain Motivation and Confidence* (Lara Honos-Webb)
◊ *ADHD and Me: What I Learned from Lighting Fires at the Dinner Table* (Blake E. S. Taylor)
◊ *Learning Outside the Lines: Two Ivy League Students With Learning Disabilities and ADHD Give You the Tools for*

Academic Success and Educational Revolution (Jonathan Mooney & David Cole)

◊ *Take Control of ADHD: The Ultimate Guide for Teens* (Ruth Spodak & Kenneth Stefano)

Once your son understands his ADHD, he can begin to learn to work through and around it. An age-appropriate explanation provides relief to many boys and affirms that they are not weird, crazy, or sick. The explanation and label can help put boundaries around your son's weaknesses so he can move forward with an attitude of hope and optimism.

Points to Consider

1. Have you accepted your son's ADHD as a disability?
2. What ADHD myths do you still believe?
3. Who will you tell about your son's ADHD, and what words will you use?
4. How will you explain ADHD to your son?

Action Steps to Take Now

1. Remember that your son has probably heard far more negative comments than positive ones. Look for areas where you can offer genuine encouragement.
2. What are your son's natural strengths or talents? List them, let him know, and post them where they are visible. Together identify one activity or experience you can provide to build upon those strengths.
3. Write a letter about your son's ADHD and deliver it to all appropriate individuals or have a discussion with the people who need to know.

4. Begin to establish a support system for yourself by enlisting the help of caring professionals (e.g., counselors, physicians, teachers), researching support groups, and continuing to read and learn about ADHD.

Chapter 2

Treatment Options for ADHD

From the day your son is born, he is learning and picking up information from his environment. If he doesn't stay focused long enough to take in, process, and store information, clearly his development will be negatively impacted. Likewise, if his behavior results in persistently negative interactions with those around him, his self-concept will suffer. As parents we must make sure supports are in place that enable him to be successful.

From our work with boys with ADHD, it appears that their behavior breaks down when the demands placed on them exceed their ability to complete the requested task. As a parent, you have seen this play out over and over. Your son may impulsively knock his head against a table when feeling frustrated with his schoolwork. He may become the class clown to avoid feeling dumb. Or, he may seem to hold himself together in school but become a little wild man at home. A recent study done by Stephanie McConaughy and colleagues (2011) showed that 15%–55% of children with ADHD "exhibited 'clinically significant' impairment in academic performance and 26–85% exhibited 'clinically significant' impairment in social behavior, depending on the measure" (p. 221). When your son can't perform, he'll let you know in a good or bad way. Your child is fortunate to have a parent like you who is concerned enough to research and learn about the best treatment options.

You know that the subject of ADHD treatment is a highly charged topic. Strong opinions run the gamut from those who believe medication is the only truly effective treatment to those who only use natural, holistic interventions, to those who support a combination of medication, environmental modification, and behavior therapy. We believe there is no one "golden nugget" treatment that fits every boy and that a combination of treatments works best.

With regard to medication, some professionals question the influence of the drug companies who manufacture the various medications. We are not medical doctors and can only speak from our own personal and professional experience and our review of the literature. Later in this chapter, we present information from a well-respected pediatrician and psychiatrist who have years of experience treating children with ADHD. The medication decision for your son needs to be grounded in your perspective along with input from teachers and others working with him. You are learning about treatment options to sort out fact from fiction.

The website for Children and Adults with Attention Deficit/ Hyperactivity Disorder (CHADD, 2011) recommended a multipronged approach to dealing with ADHD, including:

◊   parent training;
◊   behavioral intervention strategies;
◊   an appropriate educational program;
◊   education regarding ADHD; and
◊   medication, when necessary.

Starting Point

Many people who seek treatment for their son begin with their pediatrician, especially if their son has a long-standing relationship with him or her. Pediatricians have strong knowledge of developmental sequences and see children of various ages on a daily basis. However, one thing to keep in mind is that your pediatrician is seeing your son in an individualized setting where little is required of him—very different from school with children, noise, and demands to complete tasks that may be uninteresting to your child. When concerns arise, some pediatricians refer to school psychologists, clinical psychologists, neuropsychologists, neurologists, developmental pediatricians, or psychiatrists. Pediatricians are often interested in knowing the level of your son's intellectual and academic functioning as well as his executive functioning skills in order to rule out learning problems as the root cause of the behavior. Most parents are very confused about the roles of the different specialists, so a brief overview is included in Table 2.

Most pediatricians can usually treat a child with mild ADHD. A developmental pediatrician would be a good choice if your son also has complicating developmental issues such as Pervasive Developmental Disorder–Not Otherwise Specified or autism. A neurologist may be recommended if there are any concerns about brain functioning such as seizures or tics. A psychiatrist should be consulted for complicated cases where there are accompanying problems with anxiety, mood, or oppositional behavior. All of the above have gone to medical school and also can prescribe medication. A nurse practitioner usually works under the direction of a doctor and also can prescribe medication.

Clinical psychologists, neuropsychologists, and school psychologists approach ADHD from the educational, as well as the neurobiological, aspect. They focus on the impact that the behavior has on learning and general life adjustment. Their training

Table 2
Roles of Professionals in Treating ADHD

Specialty	Training	Function
Pediatrician	M.D. or D.O., general practitioner	Oversees wellness of children, diagnoses medical conditions, and prescribes medication
Developmental Pediatrician	M.D. or D.O., specialist in developmental issues	Is consulted for anomalies in development, diagnoses medical conditions, and prescribes medication
Neurologist	M.D., specialist in neurology and brain	Is consulted for neurological problems, diagnoses medical conditions, and prescribes medication
Psychiatrist	M.D., specialist in mental disorders	Is consulted for behavior/mental health issues, diagnoses conditions based on DSM-IV, and prescribes medication
Nurse Practitioner	Advanced Practice Registered Nurse (APRN)	Works under the direction of a doctor and prescribes medication
Clinical Psychologist	Ph.D. or Psy.D.	Diagnoses conditions and provides therapy, can't prescribe medication
Neuropsychologist	Ph.D. or Psy. D.	Diagnoses conditions, often does testing, can't prescribe medication
School Psychologist	Master's, specialist, Ph.D., or Psy.D.	Provides testing and consultation regarding problems that impact education, can't prescribe medication
Licensed Clinical Social Worker	MSW or Ph.D.	Diagnoses conditions and provides therapy, can't prescribe medication
Behavioral Therapist	Master's or Ph.D.	Provides behavioral therapy, can't prescribe medication

involves using various assessment measures to provide information on the child's functioning. In addition to a making a diagnosis, psychologists often rely on assessments to provide an overall picture of the child in terms of his intelligence, academic strengths and weaknesses, and processing abilities. Psychologists do not prescribe medication but often work closely with medical personnel who can. Some psychologists also provide counseling for both the individual and the family as well as behavioral therapy.

A psychologist would be a good place to start if you are unsure about the role your child's intellectual functioning plays in his behavior. For example, it is not unusual for gifted children to get into trouble at home and school because they are curious about how things work or their boredom causes misbehavior as they seek out stimulation.

Consider Malik, who was constantly in trouble with his preschool teacher. He balked at doing routine tasks that were aimed at teaching colors and shapes. He was constantly wandering around the room. When doing a standard preschool checklist, his teachers determined that he had mastered all preschool concepts. His parents made an appointment with a school psychologist for an intellectual evaluation. He scored in the gifted range and was ultimately placed in a more stimulating environment. His behavior improved instantly when he had more challenging activities and peers to interact with who were on his level.

If you are concerned about the presence of a learning disability or processing problems, a psychologist can evaluate your child's intelligence, academic skills, and processing capabilities. For example, a child may appear to be inattentive when in reality, he is not capable of doing the schoolwork he has been given and feels completely lost in the curriculum. Or a child who is not processing language may appear to have attention issues while in actuality he is not following the instructions.

This was the case with Juan, who never seemed to be doing what his kindergarten teacher asked him to do. When his group was engaged in story time, he stared around the room. When questioned about a story, his answer usually did not match the question asked. His teacher noticed that he was much more attentive when she used visuals. Juan received a comprehensive neuropsychological evaluation and was diagnosed with a learning disability as well as auditory processing problems. His behavior improved when he received special education services to remediate his learning disability and accommodate his auditory processing difficulty. From then on, his teacher always used visuals with his instruction, spoke to him in short sentences, and provided him with an example of what his finished product should look like.

Licensed clinical social workers and behavior therapists may provide therapy such as cognitive behavioral therapy, behavior modification, or family therapy. Sometimes behavior therapists work in conjunction with the classroom teacher, providing support in implementing behavior management plans designed to increase a student's motivation to comply with teacher requests and complete assigned tasks. Neither social workers nor therapists prescribe medication.

Troung's family found help from working with a therapist. He experienced more difficulty at home than at school, where the structure was much tighter. His parents experienced frequent tantrums when he did not get his way as well as dangerous, risk-taking behavior like running out into streets and climbing on furniture. They recognized that they could use some assistance in improving the way they dealt with Troung's behavior, so they contacted a therapist with training in behavior modification who assisted them in creating a more structured home environment with consequences and incentives for behavior. The therapist worked with Troung on stopping and thinking before acting, a common problem for boys with ADHD.

What the Research Says

In 1999, the National Institute of Mental Health (NIMH, 2009) released the Multimodal Treatment Study of ADHD (MTA), a study that looked at the benefits of various treatment options for nearly 600 children ages 7–9 across the country. The treatment options included:
◊ medication only,
◊ medication in conjunction with therapy,
◊ therapy only, and
◊ community care—the control group who was generally treated with lower doses of stimulant medication.

The outcomes of the study were (Pliszka & AACAP Work Group on Quality Issues, 2007):
1. Stimulant medication alone was more effective in treating ADHD than behavior-modification therapy alone.
2. The two groups of children receiving medication and those receiving medication plus behavior therapy fared better over a 14-month period than did the control group who was receiving routine community care including lower doses of medication and those receiving intensive behavioral therapy and no medication.
3. The follow-up study in 2004 showed no clear advantage to medication only as reported in the earlier study.

A follow-up (Grady, 2010) showed that the initial presentation of symptoms predicted later functioning better than the type or intensity of treatment. Thus, this large-scale research study showed long-term benefits to using a combination of medication and behavior therapy. That's what Jim and his wife did when their son was diagnosed, because they recognized that the medication helped Teddy but did not teach him any social or academic skills. At the preschool age, most practitioners agree that behavior therapy is a key part of any boy's treatment.

The NIMH also funded the Preschoolers with ADHD Treatment Study (PATS), which involved more than 300 preschoolers who had been diagnosed with ADHD. The study found that low doses of the stimulant methylphenidate were safe and effective for preschoolers but that the children were more sensitive to the side effects of the medication, including slower than average growth rates (NIH News, 2006). Therefore, preschoolers should be closely monitored by their doctor while taking ADHD medications.

Although there are some dissenting views, most physicians consider Ritalin, the drug studied in the MTA, to be effective, safe, and to have relatively few side effects. As reported by DuPaul (2007), "Numerous studies have shown methylphenidate and amphetamine compounds to improve classroom attention, behavior control, and peer interactions as well as to enhance productivity and accuracy on academic tasks and curriculum-based measurement probes" (pp. 185–186).

Treatment Is Not All About Medication

One thing to keep in mind is that ADHD is a very complex disorder with very diverse appearances and is often accompanied by other conditions such as anxiety, oppositional behavior, and/or depression. When these conditions are present, they should be addressed either through counseling, behavioral therapy, medication, or a combination of several treatment strategies. Medication does not have to be your only choice for treatment. Studies have shown that therapy in combination with medication can result in the need for lower doses of medication (Dawson, 2007). Pelham and Fabiano (2008) found in their research that treatment does not have to center around medicine when behavior modification strategies are taught to children, parents, and teachers. There is general consensus that while medication addresses symptoms, it doesn't address specific impairments such as planning, organization, and social skill deficits. Therefore, we recommend you work with a person who can see your son's complete picture and help you choose the best treatment for his unique needs.

Treatment Should Match the Need

Various studies have shown that if the correct match is made, then less intensive treatments can be as effective as more intensive ones. The goal of much of the current research is to predict which types of interventions will produce the most effective results in different types of ADHD. In other words, you want to identify your son's main challenges and then match them to the most effective treatment. Dr. Ben Vitiello (Vitiello & Sherrill, 2007) of the National Institute of Mental Health acknowledged that an important direction for research is to figure out if "it is possible to *predict* whether children with certain characteristics might benefit from certain specific treatments or to lower intensity intervention, whereas others might require different treatments or higher intensity intervention" (p. 288). Russell Barkley (2007) suggested the possibility "that different genotypes of ADHD may have different medication responses but also different responses to psychosocial treatment" (p. 284). Thus, medications and treatment for ADHD could become highly customized as more is learned about the specific genes involved.

Bottom Line

The bottom line is that one type of treatment does not work for all boys with ADHD. Because each boy has unique characteristics, his treatment needs to be comprehensive, customized, and carefully monitored. Although researchers have documented that certain treatments work for the majority of children with ADHD, there are always exceptions. You should work with a professional who takes the time to understand your son within the context of his family and school and select treatments that work for him and you. We discuss our plan, the Dynamic Action Plan, at the end of the book in the Pulling It All Together section.

Our review of research has revealed that most practitioners believe that stimulant medication is safe when prescribed and monitored by your doctor. Although promising, the research is less clear on documenting the effectiveness of other treatments, including behavioral therapy, neurofeedback, diet, and treatment for allergens. Pelham and Fabiano (2008) have noted a number of studies that show the value of behavior-related therapies and parent training. There are other, less well-known studies that appear to document the effectiveness of modifications to diet and emerging studies on neurofeedback and working memory training.

As an informed parent, it will be up to you to consider the big picture—any additional problems like academic, language, anxiety, depression, or oppositional behavior that your son may have in addition to ADHD; family stressors; and executive functioning deficits your son may have. It is important to keep in mind that medicine in general seems to be going in the direction of very individualized treatment protocols for many types of medical conditions, and ADHD is no exception. Much research is underway about specific areas of the brain impacted by ADHD, as well as studies of the effectiveness of treatments and combinations of treatments. It will be up to you and your physician as to what treatments or combinations will prove the most effective for your son.

Advice From Doctors

Because we are not medical doctors, we asked Dr. Tommy Schechtman, pediatrician, and Dr. Marshall Teitelbaum, child, adolescent, and adult psychiatrist, both in Jupiter, FL, to write about medication and ADHD.

A Pediatrician's View

We posed two questions to Dr. Schechtman.

Question 1: What questions should parents ask their pediatrician when they come in for a visit? Dr. Schechtman recommends that parents ask their pediatrician five important questions, and he also explained the importance of asking each question:

1. **What are the risks if I decide not to treat my child?**

   Everything we do in medicine should be based on constantly assessing the benefits of treatment versus potential side effects of our therapeutic interventions. Although most parents are appropriately concerned about the short-term and long-term side effects of medication, what often is not asked is, "What is the risk of not treating my son?" Not treating ADHD when it is evident can be risky. This can have a negative impact on academic performances, self-esteem, motivation, future success, and emotional stability. ADHD permeates into several areas of one's life and can impact not only your child's performance in school but, due to the impulsive nature of these individuals, can also adversely affect their social skills and personal relationships. In addition, more studies show that those who go untreated have a higher propensity to self-medicate later in life. This can take the form of substance use or addiction. Most importantly, without treatment we are depriving the child of the opportunity to meet or exceed his or her own expectations.

When we do treat a child we afford the child the ability to achieve her or his optimal success both in school and in life. When we treat a child we do not change who he is or who he wants to be but rather provide him with the "toolkit" to maximize his potential, whatever that potential is.

2. **Are there comorbidities?**

Comorbidity is the simultaneous appearance of two or more diagnoses. For example, one might meet the diagnostic criteria for ADHD and anxiety. There are several comorbidities that may appear in any individual diagnosed with ADHD. There are several other conditions that can co-occur with ADHD. The common ones include: anxiety, depression, OCD, a tic disorder, sleep disturbances, learning disabilities, and Oppositional Defiant Disorder. Some comorbidities happen alongside the diagnosis of ADHD and are separate from it. Some comorbidities are caused by the ADHD and may go away, or the symptoms may disappear when the individual is adequately treated for ADHD. When there is a separate or underlying issue in addition to the diagnosis of ADHD, this is a more complicated issue and requires a different approach to address all of the presenting issues.

3. **What happens when my child does not respond to medication?**

If your child appears to not be responding to the medication prescribed, there are several possible explanations. First of all, this may indicate that the right dose has not been achieved yet. This may require the medication be titrated up to reach optimal clinical effectiveness. Secondly, this could indicate that this is not the right type of medication. There are two forms of medication to consider in the treatment of ADHD, stimulants and nonstimulants. Stimulants have been shown to be the most clinically effective and are commonly used as a first course of treatment. If your child is experiencing severe mood changes or increased anxiety, for example, this may be an indication that there is a separate comorbidity at play that needs to be addressed and treated in addition to or separately from ADHD.

4. **How are you going to monitor my child's progress?**
   It is important to have routine periodic visits with your child's physician while he is regularly taking any form of medication. It is always important to monitor the child's growth and development as well as his vitals throughout the course of treatment. Also, we should never expect "perfect" results, but neither should you accept "good" results. Your doctor should be constantly monitoring and assessing your child's progress. Each child responds differently to different medications, and your child's regimen needs to be custom tailored for him in order to achieve "great" results.

5. **On what evidence are you basing the ADHD diagnosis?**
   Oftentimes a diagnosis of ADHD is made or assumed by an individual who is untrained or unqualified to do so. When it has been suggested to you that your child may have attention issues, make sure you address this from a comprehensive approach. Although there are several national standardized tests (e.g., Vanderbilt, Connors) for ADHD, these are not perfect assessment tools. There are not any blood or imaging (x-rays) tests or physical exam findings that help with the diagnosis. The diagnosis is one of exclusion (ruling out other neurological, physical, and psychological disorders), and one of profiling of commonly associated symptoms (e.g., lack of focus and short-term memory, poor organizational skills, impulsivity). The diagnosis needs to be made by a qualified and experienced mental health professional and/or a physician. However, because ADHD can permeate into so many areas of one's life, it

is recommended to seek the service of both. Ideally it would be best if these professionals had access to each other so that there could be the best coordination of treatment.

Question 2: As a medical doctor, how do you explain to parents how stimulants work?

Many parents are confused about how stimulants work for their already hyperactive or distracted child and they are apprehensive to use them. This is a complex decision and understandably a difficult one to make. Parents rightly should seek all of the answers they need to make a confident decision. Part of having that confidence is partnering with a physician and mental health provider who can educate you and walk with you through the diagnosis and treatment process. We try to explain the mechanics of the use of stimulant medication for the treatment of ADHD in very simplistic terms. Very simplistically, the ADHD brain craves to be stimulated, due to deficiencies or developmental issues. That is why children are so easily distracted or appear to be hyperactive. These are the ways the brain is attempting to get the stimulation it needs. When we can satisfy the brain's craving through medication, the brain can then focus on the material at hand (e.g., teacher lecturing, the book they are reading, test they are taking). ADHD does not affect one's ability or intellect. Take, for example, a child who wears glasses. We can all agree that wearing glasses does not affect the student's ability to read or her intellect. When she removes her glasses she has not lost the ability to read nor has her IQ dropped, but she can no longer read the words on the page. Her glasses are the tool her eyes need to focus on the paper she is reading or object she is looking at. In the same way, stimulant medications are a tool used to help the individual focus on the task at hand.

A Psychiatrist's View

We also posed two questions to Dr. Teitelbaum.

Question 1: Is medication for ADHD essential?

Whether medication is necessary is often perceived as controversial. Usually the decision is clinically straightforward, however. The issue is truly more one of evaluating what the true diagnoses are first, and if ADHD is either the or among the diagnoses, how the symptoms are interfering in the boy's life. If there are biologically associated diagnoses present, such as obsessive-compulsive disorder, a chronic tic disorder (including Tourette's syndrome), or bipolar disorder, then consideration has to be given toward the potential risk of using a medication for ADHD in combination with the related condition. If there are behaviorally associated comorbid conditions present, such as Oppositional Defiant Disorder, conduct disorder traits, and/or low self-esteem/depressive disorders, then the likelihood of a more aggressive measure such as using medication becomes practically essential. The bottom line is that ADHD presents differently in different folks, and how it specifically is affecting the given person is what needs to be considered the most when it comes to treatment decisions. If there are significant effects, or a near-term expectation of one or more of these, on behavioral, social, or academic function, the ADHD symptoms have to be addressed immediately. The goal is to avoid the future consequences for what happens if these problems are allowed to evolve, such as lower school and/or career achievement, higher risk for legal or substance abuse problems, more relationship challenges, and more injuries, ER visits, and moving traffic violations. In other words, we all worry about the potential risks of medications, but we also have to worry about the potential risks of not using medication. There are a number of ADHD medications available, which I will summarize below.

ADHD medications are primarily categorized into two groups, stimulants and nonstimulants. The FDA approved nonstimulants are Strattera (atomoxetine), Intuniv (long-acting guanfacine), and Kapvay or Nexiclon XR (longer-acting Clonidine formulations). These options are typically slower to take effect and less potent, although they can be used in combination with stimulants if necessary to augment treatment. All except atomoxetine are based on alpha-2 agonist blood pressure medications that have been used for years off-label to treat ADHD, but over recent years longer acting versions have come out on-label and with greater ease of use (as the prior ones often required three to four dosages per day). The alpha-2 agonists can be helpful with tic disorders, thus assisting when this genetically linked condition is part of the equation. Given the potential for blood pressure effects, they have to be increased slowly, and after having been used for a sufficient length of time, have to be reduced gradually. Atomoxetine works by way of blocking uptake on the neurotransmitter norepinephrine. Any of the medications described above can be of value if a stimulant is not considered a safe medical option or if the necessary adequate dosage of stimulant medication is not tolerable, thus sometimes requiring a combination.

The stimulant medications are the more well-known FDA approved ADHD treatments. This class is predominantly broken down into two types, those related to methylphenidate (i.e., Ritalin) or amphetamine (i.e., Adderall or Dexedrine). They all tend to cause appetite suppression, but for most children, it can be managed well with the appropriate interventions.

Methylphenidate-based medications include shorter acting (usually no more than 4 hours) and longer acting (upward of 8 hours) medications. The shorter acting medicines include methylphenidate (Ritalin) and dexmethylphenidate (Focalin).

The longer acting methylphenidates include Concerta, Ritalin LA, Metadate CD/ER, Ritalin SR, and Daytrana, along with the related dexmethylphenidate, Focalin XR. Daytrana is a patch that goes on the hip, rotating sites daily to lessen the risk of skin irritation. It can allow for better morning symptom management if applied while your son is still in bed, and can allow more active management of the wear-off time based on when it is removed, regardless of the time it is applied (e.g., if you have a teenager who likes to sleep in on weekends). Concerta, Ritalin LA, Metadate CD, and Focalin XR are medications with delivery technology that increases the likelihood of ongoing benefit throughout the day. Concerta may last longer for some, although Focalin XR may kick in faster. The times of day that require better medication coverage need to be kept in mind when using these.

Shorter acting (up to 4 hours) amphetamine-based medications (admit it, the name is scary) include Adderall (mixed dextro- and levoamphetamine salts), Dexedrine (dextroamphetamine), and ProCentra (liquid dextroamphetamine), with ProCentra being useful at times for kids who cannot swallow pills. Longer acting versions include Adderall XR, Dexedrine spansule, and Vyvanse. The longer acting medications are more likely to allow better full-day coverage, with Vyvanse being the longest acting on the average (up to 13 hours). Vyvanse is a prodrug, meaning it is turned into its active product (lisdexamfetamine into dextroamphetamine) only after the body begins to metabolize it.

As I'm prone to reminding parents, nonschool hours are often as or more important, as these can be times of higher risk. Driving while distracted can be a major danger, for instance, and the GPA is irrelevant when someone is in the emergency room.

There are a variety of other medication classes still being researched, as well as medications that are used for off-label treatment of ADHD. It is always of the utmost importance that the risks for both treating and not treating ADHD medically are fully explored to help dictate the appropriate treatment course.

Question 2: How do you know when to stop using ADHD medications with your son?

The issue of knowing if or when it might make sense to stop ADHD medication is often quite challenging to decide, especially if the boy is doing well.

There are many considerations. First, if [your son is] on a faster acting medication such as a psychostimulant, have there been days of missed dosages, and if so what transpired on these days? If the boy had a miserable day with the original symptoms of ADHD seen prior to medication initiation, in all likelihood the medication needs to be continued. If he has been doing really well for an extended time, it is usually wise to reassess the medication need at least annually, and usually at a time when it would be the least problematic if reduction causes symptom recurrence. For instance, stopping a boy's medication just prior to final exams or some other type of big event would be silly. Often lowering the dosage when there is less going on at school, and possibly with the teacher's awareness, makes it easier to assess the efficacy. Other times it can be less risky to reduce when school is out, although if the main issues of ADHD are on the inattentive (vs. impulsive) spectrum, it can be more challenging to evaluate.

The most important issues have to do whether the symptoms of ADHD are still there, which is usually the case to at least some degree for the majority of affected individuals, and what ways the residual symptoms are still interfering. A boy who has problems with socialization or behavior when off of medication is likely to have a variety of problems if taking an extended break from medication over the summer, for instance.

If he is either having no further life interferences without medication or is having minimal enough disturbance that can be addressed in other ways (e.g., organizational coaching, psychotherapy), then it may be reasonable to stop medication.

It is hard being a parent. It is even harder when you have a son with ADHD, as often you do not get the support of others like you do with a child with other medical problems. However, it is your responsibility to make the decisions that are in the best interest of your child, regardless of whether they are easy or popular. I often compare the condition to severe allergy or vision problems, as none are thought of as immediately life threatening, but the quality of life and potential risks going forward, if ignored, can be severe. If the medical issue is interfering with your son's life, then it is your responsibility as a parent to make decisions, even those that you do not like. Keep in mind that your son is not choosing to have ADHD (i.e., be distracted, disorganized, hyperactive). So, take advantage of all of the resources that this modern society has to offer!

Thanks to Drs. Schechtman and Teitelbaum for sharing their valuable insight with us. We acknowledge that it's not often that a parent is afforded the time during their son's doctor's visit to hear this type of information because many doctors are pressed for time. And even if we had the time to hear this from a doctor, it would be too much to quickly take in, so it is nice to have an explanation in writing to read and reference as needed.

Cautions About Medication

Parents have a myriad of concerns about medication, including decreased appetite, stunting of growth, medication becoming addictive, and recent concerns about heart problems. We had these concerns ourselves, and from our experiences as parents, we acknowledge that medications did impact our sons' sleep, appetite, and moods as the drug wore off. Jim and his wife grappled with the medication's side effects and ultimately concluded that the discomfort of the side effects was worth the gain they saw in Teddy. As Teddy once told Jim, "I don't want to take my medication, but it helps me concentrate." If your child is or may soon be taking medication, an honest discussion with your doctor is important so he or she can explain the cautions and help you feel comfortable with your decision. There's no doubt that you have already been influenced by the media, family, and friends, so it is important to know you have considered the best available advice and made the best decision for your son. Ask your doctor some of the insightful questions discussed in this chapter. Finally, if you choose medication, be assured that there is much research to back up its benefits and safety when it is prescribed judiciously and carefully monitored by you and your physician.

Really, Should I Medicate My Son?

As concerned parents ourselves, we are presenting the facts to you as straightforward as we can, and we are not trying to lead you in either direction. It's your decision. Our perception is that mainstream media portrays ADHD medication in an unfavorable way when the reality is that medication helps a lot of boys have the opportunity to work up to their potential. We know this from our professional and personal experiences.

Jim and his wife were confronted with the above question when Teddy was diagnosed at age 6. They asked themselves, "Should we medicate our 6-year-old?" They considered two main factors before making the decision to try medication. First, Teddy was aware that he was getting in trouble from his teacher. Second, his inability to concentrate was affecting his learning and he was falling behind in reading. After consulting with the pediatrician, a medication trial was started. Right away Teddy's teacher noticed an improvement in his behavior and schoolwork. At the time, Jim's wife ate lunch with Teddy at school on Fridays. The Friday after he started the medication she was helping in the class and a student spontaneously said, "Teddy's mom, he hasn't been getting in trouble lately." Even his peers noticed the improvement. So, despite initial hesitations, medication helped Teddy improve his confidence and academics.

When to Stop Medication

Dr. Teitelbaum provided some good advice for you to consider, and here we add our personal touch. Jim and his wife had Teddy taking a type of medication that allowed him not to take it on weekends, holidays, or during the summer. They decided to stop having him take any medication near the end of his fifth-grade year. They considered the following points when deciding when to stop ADHD medication.

◊   Was he mature enough to try going without medication?
◊   Were the side effects of medication worth the benefit?
◊   How were his grades?
◊   How was his school and home behavior?
◊   What was he saying about how it helped?
◊   What was he like when the medication wore off?
◊   If he stopped now, would he have to start again later?
◊   What did the medical doctor say about stopping?

We suggest that you consider these and your own points. During this process one thing we typically advise parents against doing is stopping medication just because your son puts up a fuss when it is time to take his medication or if he complains that he doesn't want to take it anymore. Boys can be compelling and badgering, but this alone is not a valid reason to cease treatment. We recommend that there be a medical reason or several compelling reasons to stop.

Your Son's Diet

There is no question that children with and without ADHD will benefit from a well-balanced diet of proteins, fats, and carbohydrates, as well as adequate vitamins and minerals. The natural foods movement has been gaining momentum for all people. However, there is significant controversy about the role of diets in children with ADHD. There are proponents of elimination diets and/or supplementation with nutrients as treatments for ADHD, neither of which have wide research support but have anecdotal support. If you choose any of these elimination or supplementary diet approaches, it will be important to first discuss it with your pediatrician. The National Resource Center on ADHD (2008) provided a discussion of complementary and alternative treatments and warned readers that "the FDA does not strictly regulate the ingredients or the manufacturer claims about dietary supplements. Go to the FDA web site to learn about existing regulations" (para. 27).

The Feingold Diet, developed during the 1960s by Ben Feingold, a San Francisco allergist, focuses on eliminating "artificial flavorings, preservatives, dyes, and other additives, as well as food containing naturally occurring salicylates (such as oranges, apples, apricots, berries, and grapes" (Armstrong, 1995, p. 72) However, most studies have not verified the effectiveness of the diet, even though anecdotal reports indicate some children with sensitivities to these substances have benefited from it. We don't recommend this diet.

If you feel that your child may be sensitive to food additives, you might want to keep a log of food your child is eating and note adverse effects. Many doctors recommend 2 weeks on and 2 weeks off for any substance you are checking for sensitivities. Monitor any specific behavior changes in your son during that time and report them to your doctor or other professional.

Neurofeedback/Biofeedback

Neurofeedback (also called EEG biofeedback or biofeedback) is a type of brain exercise or training and is an alternative treatment for ADHD that is gaining research validity. For instance, researchers at Ohio State University have National Institute of Mental Health funding and have completed a pilot study on neurofeedback. Based on their pilot study, the results were promising enough for them to launch a large scale, multisite research study (personal communication, E. Arnold, M.D., February 4, 2011). These types of large-scale neurofeedback studies serve to further inform parents about its effectiveness. Currently there are limited large-scale research studies on neurofeedback and most have small sample sizes. Many neurofeedback studies have been conducted by researchers outside of the United States. Within the United States, some studies report positive results for using neurofeedback to treat individuals with ADHD. Readers interested in the specific neurofeedback literature are referred to the work of Monastra and colleagues (Monastra, 2004; Monastra et al., 2005; Monastra, Monastra, & George, 2002), as they provide a good starting point. It was reported in some of Monastra's (Monastra et al., 2002) studies that EEG biofeedback was a promising treatment for ADHD when used as part of a multimodal treatment approach of parent counseling, EEG biofeedback, and stimulant therapy and that more research was needed. In their 2005 study, Monastra and colleagues concluded:

> Although it is clear from the outcomes of each of
> the published cases and controlled studies of EEG
> biofeedback for ADHD, that significant, beneficial

effects have consistently been reported in patients/ families who volunteered to receive this type of treatment, additional controlled, group studies (with random assignment to treatment condition) are needed in order to promote a clearer under- standing of the number of patients and degree of improvement that can be anticipated in clinical practice. (p. 108)

The premise behind how neurofeedback works is that a per- son's brain rhythms are either working too fast or too slow. Thus, neurofeedback training helps a person modify his brain's rhythms or electrical activity. While participating in a neurofeedback ses- sion, the boy's brain rhythms are recorded using EEG technology. Depending on the neurofeedback practitioner, the boy either has electrodes attached to his scalp or he wears a special cap that con- tains electrodes. These electrodes record the boy's brain activity as he engages in a computer-based activity that teaches him how to alter his brain rhythms. The goal is to teach the boy how to become aware of and modify his brain rhythms with the goal of normalizing them. Normalized brain rhythms should lead the boy to have sustained benefits that translate into improved behavior and schoolwork.

Jim and his wife believed neurofeedback had enough validity behind it, so they had their son partake in about 30 neurofeed- back sessions. At the time Teddy started neurofeedback, he was 10 years old and halfway through his fifth-grade year. He had been taking ADHD medication since kindergarten. While taking an extended-release ADHD medication, his mornings went well, but it was harder for him to concentrate and complete his schoolwork during the afternoon. Before beginning neurofeedback, they con- sulted with his teacher and she supported the decision and agreed to help by monitoring his performance. Teddy continued taking his ADHD medication as he progressed through the neurofeedback sessions. Overall, his teacher reported an improvement in his ability to concentrate, stay on task in the morning, and complete his class work, but she did not notice any improvement during the afternoon. Jim and his wife did not notice any significant improvement at home.

Working Memory Training

We believe working memory training programs are promising emerging alternative treatments for boys with ADHD. Dr. Russell Barkley (1997) identified working memory as one of four key neuropsychological components of his model for ADHD (the others are self-regulation, internalization of speech, and reconstitution). Other researchers have supported the importance of working memory in a child's ability to remain attentive (Alderson, Rapport, Hudec, Sarver, & Kofler, 2010; Kofler, Rapport, Bolden, Sarver, & Raiker, 2010).

Of the available working memory programs, we recommend Cogmed Working Memory Training because of the solid independent research supporting its effectiveness. At this time there are numerous independently published research studies that provide evidence regarding the effectiveness of the Cogmed Working Memory Training to help children with ADHD improve working memory and behavior (Holmes et al., 2009; Mezzacappa & Bucker, 2010; Rief, 2008) and improve word reading and reading comprehension in children with special needs (Dahlin, 2011).

The Cogmed Working Memory Training is an Internet-based computer software program that the child completes at home. One of the Cogmed program's top features is that this program is only licensed to a psychologist or medical doctor. Second, each child's performance is monitored weekly by a quality assurance coach. It is a 5 week, 5-day-a-week program that the child completes on his own or with parent supervision. Each session ranges from

35–45 minutes and as the child finishes each working memory activity, his performance is recorded within the Cogmed software. The software is self-adjusting so that the child works within his instructional zone. The quality assurance coach checks in with the parent once a week, reviews the child's performance, and offers suggestions for improvement. After the child completes the 5-week regiment, there are regular booster sessions and follow-up from the coach.

Allergies and ADHD

If you suspect your son has ADHD, then a comprehensive evaluation should be completed to rule out various conditions that look like ADHD. For example, if a boy has allergies, then they can affect his concentration, memory, or ability to focus. Many parents are concerned about allergies to red food dye. If your son's evaluation is with a medical doctor, then the doctor will take a thorough history in order to determine if allergies could be involved. If you or your doctor strongly suspects your son may have allergies, then blood work will be requested to make an official decision.

In our experiences, having blood work done is the preferred procedure for allergy testing, and Jim learned this the hard way. Because of a person's testimony, Jim had his son tested for allergies using a nonmedical practitioner who did not use blood work as part of the procedure. Jim heard from the principal of Teddy's elementary school that there was another young boy in the school with ADHD. One summer the boy's parents took him to a homeopathic allergist for a series of treatments. The principal reported that the next school year the child was like a different kid in terms of the behaviors related to ADHD.

Jim and his wife wanted that for Teddy too. They researched the type of approach the other family used on the Internet. A website reported that ADHD can be treated with a natural approach from an allergist. The closest practitioner to their home was a 45-minute drive each way, but they thought it could be worthwhile.

At the first appointment, the practitioner explained the procedures, and Jim and his wife asked him questions about his success rate in treating young patients with ADHD. He said many of his patients had fewer symptoms after several treatments. Teddy went through the homeopathic allergy testing and the practitioner found he was allergic to calcium, soy, and egg. They decided to treat the soy first so Teddy went through the natural treatment procedure, which involved pressure points and not having Teddy ingest or contact any soy product for 24 hours.

After numerous trips and sessions they accomplished the treatment for soy and calcium but did not see any noticeable change in Teddy's behavior at home or school. They discontinued the treatments and were out $500. In hindsight, Jim believes they first should have taken Teddy to a medical doctor for allergy testing.

Counseling

Many boys with ADHD find help working with a counselor or mental health therapist. Although counseling does not cure ADHD, it can teach boys how to better manage their ADHD. Counseling helps boys whether or not they are taking ADHD medication. We like to use the saying, "Pills don't teach skills." Boys taking ADHD medications still need to learn how to harness their strengths and work with their ADHD. Medication alone won't teach your son the valuable life skills he'll need for success, so that's why counseling can be an effective treatment. Because each boy is unique, your son will have his own specific needs. Many boys use counseling to learn how to develop and maintain a positive mindset, appropriately express their frustrations, or deal with anger. What skills could your son use help developing?

In our experiences, parents typically seek counseling when they feel like they have done everything they know how to do, yet there are still problems. When your son's challenges reach crisis level, it may prompt you to reach out for a professional's support. As one mom told us, "I just couldn't take one more phone call from the school telling me about his bad behavior. I had to do something." As school psychologists, we become the "do something" as parents turn to us for parenting guidance. To have the most benefit, counseling usually involves you, your son, and the immediate family.

There are various counseling methods. In our practices, we provide a limited amount of counseling, but when we do, we apply the principles of cognitive behavioral therapy. We prefer using cognitive behavioral therapy because it presumes that a boy's thoughts, not external events or people, cause his feelings and behaviors. Thus, we try to change his behavior by changing his thoughts. Cognitive behavioral therapy has a solid research base and is short term, goal oriented, and instructive. During counseling, boys are taught how to identify and express concerns, problem solve, and apply what they learned. The sessions also involve the boy evaluating how well he applied the newly learned skill. As part of the counseling process, parents also learn how to change their thoughts and behavior.

In our work, parents and boys tell us this type of counseling is usually helpful for making meaningful life changes. For instance, many adolescent boys with ADHD have lost their academic motivation by middle school. When parents and teachers come to us for help we often hear them describe the boy as unmotivated, lazy, not applying himself, or having no interest in school. We have helped boys individually and in small groups to improve their academic motivation. One helpful book we use to structure these types of counseling sessions is *Enhancing Academic Motivation: An Intervention Program for Young Adolescents* by Norman Brier. This book contains 16 lessons that each include goal setting, discussion, role-plays, and homework. The homework is important to help boys follow through after the counseling session. This program also has a parent component so parents can reinforce the information their son has learned. We believe this program works well because its format is not what a boy typically thinks about when he hears he is going to counseling. Most boys perceive counseling as it is seen in the movies, with the patient lying on a sofa talking to a counselor. This book's lessons are interactive and engage boys in a way that seems to make the time pass quickly. We've found that many boys who are initially reluctant to participate in counseling end up looking forward to the sessions.

A secret to making counseling work for you and your son is finding the right match between your son and his counselor. Having a strong relationship will make or break how well his counseling works. Therefore it is very important to talk to the counselor about this from the start. You should know after three or four sessions if it's the right pairing. Ask your son questions such as, "How do you like the counselor? Do you feel like he or she listens and understands you? Are you becoming comfortable talking to him or her?" Likewise, ask the counselor if your son is expressive, open, and honest. From this point you can make the decision to stay or find another counselor. These are questions to ask when choosing a counselor for your son:

◇ What is your philosophy toward helping make meaningful change?
◇ What type of counseling is used?
◇ Is there a specific curriculum?
◇ How long does the average client remain in counseling?
◇ What are common causes for leaving?
◇ What is the most frequent age range of boy you counsel?
◇ How are parents and/or family involved?
◇ Does the counselor communicate with teachers or school staff?

To summarize, counseling is a proven way for your son to learn important life skills for managing his ADHD and building a skill set for life. One parent of an 8-year-old told us, "I feel lost as a parent. I feel like I can't get control of his behavior. He's out of control, I'm not in control, and I'm not sure how to rein in his behavior." In this case, Joey's behavior was much worse at home than at school because he responded to the tightly structured environment provided for him at school and had strong academic skills. His family was reluctant to engage in family therapy but realized they had no other choice if they were to help Joey. His parents were not organized people themselves but realized they had to "tighten up" their ship, provide consistency, and hold Joey accountable for his behavior. It went against their nature to be so scheduled, but they knew it was what Joey needed. They found that the techniques they had used when he was younger no longer worked, so they had to acquire new tools and strategies. They learned to provide necessary cues and prompts to guide behavior, which of course didn't always work. In those instances, they had to learn new ways to deal with the misbehavior. As Dr. Harold Koplewicz (1996) stated, "The message a parent must convey to children who misbehave is: This is unacceptable behavior. It will not be tolerated. It keeps you from functioning in the world" (p. 85). The goal is to help children with ADHD learn to stay calm and in control and have a plan in place to help them manage their impulsivity and avoid situations that bring on misbehavior.

Coaching

Coaching involves assistance with tasks such as organization, scheduling, goal setting, and time management. Teenagers and adults are the most likely candidates to find success with coaching. Coaching is often more action oriented than counseling. The coach will often assist the person with ADHD in breaking down tasks into short-term goals and will check in frequently to see how the person is progressing toward those goals.

Nancy Ratey and Susan Sussman have established the National Coaching Network and a formalized curriculum for coaching adults with ADHD. Many of their strategies can also be used in coaching children and teenagers with ADHD. Their plan involves self-evaluation to assess strengths and weaknesses, including whether the person responds to visual or auditory reminders and the creation and monitoring of a plan to manage needed changes (see Ratey, 2008, for more information).

Parent Training

If you are like most parents of boys with ADHD, you cannot even begin to count the times you have thrown your hands up in dismay at the daunting task of parenting. You want the best for your son but are at a loss as to how to make that happen. Dr. Phyllis Teeter (1998), author of *Interventions for ADHD: Treatment in Developmental Context*, suggested that parent training will be essential, especially to increase the likelihood that your child will comply with your rules and structure.

She discussed three major parent-training programs from Barkley, Patterson, and Forehand and McMahon. All three "incorporate techniques to improve parent-child interactions, to decrease noncompliance and to facilitate family communication patterns" Teeter, 1998, p. 155). The overall benefit to parent training has been difficult to document through research studies, but our experience has been that it is always of some benefit when parents can improve their skills, even in one area. How many times have you wished for just one skill that would make you feel like you had some impact on your son's behavior?

General Behavior Strategies

In upcoming chapters, we will discuss behavioral techniques that have proven successful with various age groups. We will stress the importance of structure, predictable and consistently administered consequences, an environment engineered for success, and positive support for all age groups. Listed below are specific behavioral strategies you may also want to implement that we have found useful with our sons and clients.

Establishing Clear, Firm Boundaries

One of the secrets of effectively parenting boys with ADHD is to provide clear and firm boundaries for what types of behaviors are and are not acceptable in your home. If you don't establish and continually remind your son about these acceptable behaviors, he will take advantage of you and his siblings, and you will find yourself yelling at your children and feeling like they don't listen or respect you. This is when we often receive calls from our clients seeking help. Here's what we recommend. Create this plan with your spouse or other adult(s) in the home who will be helping to implement the plan. You want everyone on the same page and consistent.

1. Identify and write down your five most important rules.
2. Write down the consequences for not following the rules (e.g., first infraction, second, third).
3. Schedule a family meeting.
4. Discuss the rules and consequences and clarify expectations.
5. Implement the new plan.

When deciding on your five most important rules, try to keep them short. For example, rules in Jim's home include: no cursing, no name calling, keep hands and feet to yourself, no talking back, and complete assigned chores. His consequences include a verbal warning, time in your room, loss of privileges (e.g., video games, phone, computer, driving), and grounding. When Jim's son with ADHD is grounded, it means he can't play any videogames, watch TV, use the computer, or see or talk with friends. He is allowed to read, draw, or play outside by himself.

As you sit everyone down for the family meeting, structure the conversation by saying something similar to this:

> You may have noticed that things have not been running so smoothly in our family lately and there has been a lot of yelling and arguing. It's time to get our family back on the right track and get us working together as a team. After all, if we don't take care of our family, who will? No "super nanny" is going to show up on our doorstep, so it's up to us to make our home run smoother. We need and want everyone to contribute his or her fair share, so we came up with these new rules. We've always had family rules, but they might not have been so clear. Now we've clearly listed them along with the consequences of not following them. Let's go over them together so we are all on the same page.

By having this type of talk and agreement with your family, you have just removed some of the emotion that will occur the next time you discipline your son or other children. The clear consequences help you remain neutral because everyone has agreed upon the rules and consequences. So if your son decides to curse, you can confidently state the warning and inform him that the next consequence results in a loss of a privilege. Expect your son to test you on the new rules and consequences for two reasons. First, he is impulsive and he will know the rule but won't consider it before acting and breaking the rule. Second, he wants to test you to find out if you are serious about enforcing the rules. This plan will work, but as we've stated before, you must be consistent in using it and following through.

Using Behavior Plans

Behavior charts and plans also work to modify a boy's behavior when used consistently. In our experiences, parents are challenged to maintain and monitor the plans over time. Most parents start out strong and then fizzle out within a week or two. Although it's beyond the scope of this book to provide behavioral charts and plans, we do want to explain the basics of using behavior plans at home.

Jim used behavior plans with his son while he was in kindergarten and first grade. Although he did not use them continually throughout these two grades, he faded them in and out as needed. Behavior plans work well for children who do not yet have the natural ability to self-monitor their own behavior. As described in Chapter 3, young boys with ADHD are not able to self-reflect well, so they benefit from the external control that a behavior plan provides.

Jim identified and wrote 10 important behaviors on Teddy's behavior plans. At the end of each day, Jim reviewed each behavior with his son. If his son followed the individual behavior, then Jim drew a smiley face in the square, but if his son did not follow the behavior, then Jim drew a sad face. Each day his son needed to get 8 out of 10 smiley faces in order to earn a reward. At the end of the week, if he had 4 out of 5 days with 8 or more smiley faces, then he picked a larger reward from the prize box that Jim and his wife created. This external control and reinforcement helped Jim's son improve his school behavior.

Incorporating the Element of Time

We have found that many younger boys with ADHD improve their performance when they are challenged with the element of time or provided with a game-like atmosphere for completing tasks. Some boys like to do things fast and within a certain amount of time. For example you might say, "I'm going to time you to see how fast you can pick up your clothes off the floor and put them in the clothes hamper. Ready? Go!" The element of time and necessity motivates them to complete tasks and this helps explain why using a timer works with many boys.

Motivating with visual timers. We recommend using a visual timer that a boy can view. A simple kitchen timer, microwave timer, or an app for your smart phone all work well. Give your son a reasonable amount of time to complete his task and set the timer. If he has to write spelling sentences, say, "Let's see if you can write five good sentences using neat handwriting in 15 minutes. Do you think you can do it? Remember, the sentences must be good and neat. Go." Teachers can use timers in the classroom with your young son. You or the teacher can purchase small timers that fit on a desk. When it's time for your son to complete independent seatwork, he can set the timer for the designated time. This provides him with a visual reminder to remain on task. Timers are a versatile tool that can help him at home or school.

Utilizing a game format. We find that some young boys with ADHD complete tasks better when part of the task is turned into a game-like experience. If your son resists when you tell him it is time to take a bath, then make a game about getting to the tub. Ask him if he can hop like a bunny to the bathroom. Can he crawl like a turtle or lumber like an elephant? Many boys enjoy the novelty and readily comply. We've seen teachers apply this concept within the classroom by asking the class to line up from tallest to shortest or vice versa. Other teachers encourage their students to walk in line by having them walk with their hands in their pockets, hands folded behind their backs, or one hand behind their backs and one in front of them. Again, this provides novelty. We caution you that this strategy works but not if you use the activity over and over. You must use your creativity and vary the game. So, the next time your son whines when you ask him to complete a simple task, try altering it into a novel game-like experience.

Offering the Two-Seat Method

Think back to the last time you took a class or seminar where you had to study for a test. Where did you like to study? Was it on your bed, at a desk, sitting at the kitchen table, or on your comfy couch? We bet there were at least two places where your concentrated and studied best. Those two places had the right feeling to get you into study mode. The same goes for the boy with ADHD, and this is the premise behind the two-seat method. Sometimes it feels best to have the choice between two places to complete school- or homework. If you like this idea and your son is eligible for accommodations, then you can have the two-seat method written into his IEP or 504 plan. Then, he will have the choice of sitting at his desk or in another location, such as an empty table in the back of the room, to do his work. At home you can provide him with the choice of working at a table or another designated spot. Providing your son with choices helps empower him and may allow him to create better work.

Providing Choices

Which do you prefer, waking up early or sleeping in? Working in the evening or working in the early morning? Getting paid once a month or every other week? People like choices, and the same holds true for boys with ADHD. As parents we found our sons usually responded better when presented with two choices. For example, we've given choices such as, "You can cut the grass in the morning or after lunch, but it will be cut today," "You can wear this shirt to school or this one," "You can learn to play the piano or guitar," and "Would you like to do your spelling words now or right after dinner?" Giving your son choices does not excuse him from the task.

Think about what providing choices does for him. First, it helps him learn to problem solve. For instance, if he is presented with the choice of vacuuming out the car on Saturday before or after he watches a favorite cartoon, then he must think about the benefits. If he completes the task before his show, then he does not have to think about it and can enjoy the show. Yet, vacuuming before the show starts could take longer than anticipated, and then he'd miss part of the show. Waiting until after the show presents a different set of potential problems. Even though this seems like a simple decision, it requires him to apply problem-solving skills.

Next, providing choices helps your son learn to make decisions. Some boys become indecisive because choices are made for them. As parents we should provide our sons with age-appropriate decision-making opportunities. If choices are made for him as a child, then your son may mature into an adult who can't make his own decisions. He may be easily swayed into unhealthy habits or relationships.

Finally, giving your son choices can help empower him and make him feel valued. One birthday Teddy was given the choice of celebrating his birthday by spending the night at a local dude ranch with his grandparents and cousins or having a party with lots of friends at a local venue. He chose the family birthday celebration at the dude ranch, and the weekend turned out fantastic, with many laughs and memories. He felt great about the decision, and everyone thanked him for inviting them.

The main points to remember are that you want your son to learn to problem solve and to make his own good choices. In order to do that, he needs three things from you: opportunity, instruction, and helpful feedback. You can get started today.

Giving Second Chances

We strongly urge you not to get into an "all or nothing" situation with your son when it comes to behavior. He should be given a way to "earn it back," or else he has nothing to work for and will often refuse to do anything or just act out because he now has nothing to lose. For example, we observed a teacher tell a boy during independent seatwork that he had 5 minutes to complete a set of math problems or he'd be staying in to work during recess. She did this to try to motivate the boy to work faster, but it backfired on her. He stayed on task but did not complete the problems, so his teacher told him he'd lost his recess time. He became belligerent and refused to do any more work, made noises, and distracted others. The teacher then gave him more consequences that he did not care about because he had already lost out on his favorite part of the school day. When he continued to disrupt the class, the teacher, in desperation, sent him to the office. The teacher could have avoided this by saying something like, "I see you did not get the required work completed, so you can have 5 more minutes to complete it or a 5-minute recess delay so you can try to finish up." Now the boy understands that he still gets to enjoy recess but may have a slight delay. Most boys can handle that.

Points to Consider

1. When deciding on treatment, do you have a good understanding of your son's strengths and weaknesses? This will be very important as treatment becomes more individualized.
2. What choices do you provide your son in his day-to-day life?

3. Could your son benefit from neurofeedback or working memory training?

Action Steps to Take Now

1. Write down your own plan to determine the best treatment or combination of treatments for your son.
2. Decide which professionals need to be involved in helping your son reach his full potential.
3. Determine which topics need to be the subject of further research for you.
4. Learn more about neurofeedback or working memory training.
5. Which one behavioral strategy can you apply or try again?

Chapter 3

Infancy and Preschool

Your bouncing baby boy is wearing you to a frazzle. He is charming, yet he is constantly demanding adult attention, running from one activity to another, and having meltdowns at the slightest provocation. You may feel like he is running your life. You have stopped inviting friends and relatives to your home because you are embarrassed about his behavior. You are tired of being accused of being a bad parent.

Like most parents of boys, you knew to expect boundless energy and lots of activity. However, you are exhausted and are sure your son's activity level is abnormally high. Perhaps you have already been told he has ADHD.

It is important to remember that organization, thinking before acting, and being able to sustain attention are all developmental by nature, meaning that behaviors can occur within a range of ages and still be considered within the normal range. Parents often wonder how it is possible to distinguish typical behavior appropriate to the developmental stage from atypical ADHD behaviors and how long it should take their son to progress through developmental stages. Dr. Russell Barkley (2000b) reported that research has shown that a majority (57%) of 4-year-olds may be rated as inattentive and overactive by their parents. However, the majority of these children improve within 3–6 months. Even among those children who received a clinical diagnosis of ADHD, only half maintained that diagnosis through later childhood and adolescence. He notes that when the "pattern of ADHD lasts for at least a year, ADHD will likely continue into later childhood" (p. 91). The lesson that we can take from this information is that the severity of ADHD symptoms and length of time they last predict which children will show a chronic course of ADHD.

Keath Low (2009), writer for the ADD/ADHD Guide at About.com, suggested some questions to consider:

◇ How does your son's activity level and behavior compare to those of boys of the same age? (Remember that even a period of months can mean big developmental leaps, so comparing your son to boys very close in age is important.)

◇ Is his behavior more extreme and disruptive than that of other boys his age?

◇ Does your son have ongoing problems in daily life activities?

◇ Do the behavioral difficulties occur in more than one setting (such as home and preschool or play groups)?

◇ Could the behavior be caused by other factors and conditions, or do you believe it is innate or inborn?

When Is a Comprehensive Evaluation Warranted?

A preschooler who puts himself in danger by being overactive, distracted, or impulsive and who has difficulty with daily activities such as eating, playing with friends, attending preschool, and interacting in the community merits comprehensive evaluation. The chances of a child like this growing out of this level of behavior without intervention is slim. The more knowledgeable you are about the disorder, the more you can help your son.

The moment he enters any room, 4-year-old Ian begins scanning the area. His eyes dart from one area to the next and his body follows suit as if he cannot fully take in one thing before his racing mind pulls him to the next. In fact, he has run into the street on several occasions and requires constant supervision. He talks nonstop in a shrill voice and has no idea about volume control. He is engaging and friendly with adults. In fact, he demands almost constant adult attention and interaction except when he is glued to the computer screen playing a game. He will not sit still for family meals and generally has his home in an uproar. He is no longer invited to some homes to play and has been asked to leave his first preschool. Ian is clearly a candidate for a comprehensive evaluation, including a thorough developmental history, reports and/or ratings of his behavior in different settings, and a neuropsychological and/or medical examination to rule out other conditions.

Awareness and early detection enable you to have a better understanding of your child's behaviors. The preschool years are an important window of time in development. Your son will need you to be his advocate and safety net as he explores his world and adapts to the structure of a preschool setting.

ADHD has been diagnosed in children as young as 2 and is the "most common mental health diagnosis for children ages 3 to 5," according to the *Harvard Mental Health Letter* (Harvard Health Publications, 2007, para. 1). It is being recognized at earlier and earlier ages for several reasons. More is known about the condition, and boys are beginning "school readiness activities at earlier ages" in preschool programs (Wolraich, 2007, p. 9). These programs bring new demands in terms of compliance, attention and focus, and behavioral control. It can be a time of great stress for parents as they struggle to find answers and interventions for their son's behavior or find and locate an appropriate preschool, all while managing their own personal and professional lives. Parents often tell us that parenting preschoolers with ADHD has been one of their biggest challenges but also a time of great satisfaction as they watch their children mature.

Prenatal Issues

As noted in an earlier chapter, it is important to put aside any parental guilt if your son has ADHD. The latest research reported in *The Lancet*, a British medical journal (Williams, 2010), has shown that children with ADHD have a larger number of DNA segments that are either duplicated or missing, known as copy number variants. Genetically based neurological characteristics, including less activity in the frontal regions of the brain (especially those areas that inhibit behavior, resist distractions, and control activity level) and differences in the effectiveness of neurotransmitters, have been suggested. Although home environment plays a role in improving or worsening a child's temperament, it does not cause true ADHD. Because it is genetic, it is possible that you or your mate has ADHD.

In addition to the genetic link, risk factors can be increased by (Barkley, 2000b; Goldstein, 1999):

◇ prematurity and significantly low birth weight;
◇ prenatal exposure to alcohol, tobacco, and illegal drugs;
◇ complications of the fetus that interfere with normal brain development;
◇ excessively high lead levels; and
◇ postnatal injury to the prefrontal regions of the brain.

Many parents of boys with ADHD state unequivocally that they have known since before birth that their child had an abnormal activity level. A 4-year-old diagnosed with ADHD was described by his mother as a "kicking machine" in the womb. She said, "He was raring to go from the start."

Developmental Issues: Birth and Beyond

According to the Perinatal Collaborative Project (discussed in Barkley, 2000b), some features in the early development of children predict a greater risk of development of ADHD, even though the risks are reported to be low. These risk factors include (Barkley, 2000b):

◇ smaller head size at birth,
◇ amniotic fluid stained by meconium (intestinal material from the fetus),
◇ signs of nerve damage and/or breathing problems after birth, and
◇ delays in motor development.

Developmental Sequences

Educating yourself about what to expect at different age levels is important for any parent, especially if you have a bouncing bundle of energy on your hands. These characteristics have been shown to be common in children later diagnosed with ADHD (Bailey, 2009):

Infancy (0–12 months):

◇ Very high activity level, constantly moving
◇ Little interest in cuddling
◇ Low frustration tolerance, impatient, and highly demanding of caretakers
◇ Intense reactions to stimulation
◇ Highly attention seeking

Toddler (1–3 years):
- ◊ Difficulty maintaining attention for even several minutes
- ◊ Distracted by noise or visual stimuli
- ◊ Poor eye contact
- ◊ Ability to pay attention to things he is really interested in such as video games
- ◊ Excessively active
- ◊ Lack of interest in quiet activities
- ◊ Difficulty regaining control when excited
- ◊ Highly impulsive and risk taking
- ◊ Accident prone
- ◊ Difficulty sleeping, either falling asleep and/or waking early

Preschool (3–5 years):
- ◊ Can't sit still
- ◊ Little interest in quiet activities, such as looking at books or listening to stories
- ◊ Limited task persistence, changing tasks every few minutes
- ◊ Inconsistent attention skills, especially between preferred and nonpreferred activities
- ◊ Weak social skills
- ◊ Behavioral problems, disobedience, and engaging in unsafe behaviors
- ◊ Very talkative
- ◊ Constant motion such as running without looking
- ◊ Clumsy or poor coordination
- ◊ Difficulty waiting a turn
- ◊ Aggression such as hitting other children or grabbing items from them

Consideration of Wide Variations in Normal Developmental Sequences

Developmentally, many children begin acquiring the ability to inhibit behavior at 3 years and can voluntarily direct their attention to a nonpreferred task at 4 years (Wendling, 2008). However, the developmental sequence can vary widely and still be considered to be within the normal range. Some 4-year-old girls can sit and color for 2 hours, while very few 4-year-old boys can sit for that long. Gender differences have been widely documented. Preschool girls are much more prone than boys to enjoy sedentary activities such as coloring and looking at books. Any observer of preschool boys can attest to their boundless energy and rambunctious play.

Again, it is important to understand that attention and focus are developmental in nature and do not occur at the same time for all children. Developmental readiness determines what a child is able to do at any point in time. It cannot be rushed. Educate yourself about developmental stages and what you can realistically expect at various ages, taking into account gender and developmental differences.

Importance of Ruling Out Other Causes of Behavior

As a preschooler, your son will be very busy asserting his independence and will be exuberant as he explores his surroundings. A hallmark of the "terrible twos" is disruptive behavior, especially when overtired or overstimulated. These characteristics and a number of other developmental issues make ADHD difficult to diagnose in preschoolers. These include an overlap between symptoms of ADHD and other conditions, differences in parenting skills and childhood experiences that could exacerbate the condition, and especially the wide variation in normal developmental sequences.

Parents of boys are acutely aware that boys often trail girls in meeting many developmental milestones, especially in language, fine motor skills, and the ability to sit and engage in quiet activities.

A cautionary factor for physicians and psychologists in diagnosing ADHD in preschoolers is that symptoms can mimic other conditions such as anxiety, depression, behavioral disorders, hearing or vision problems, sensory issues, developmental delays, language processing problems, or lead exposure. It is important to rule out other factors, especially if that knowledge leads to effective interventions.

For example, Jamie had fine motor delays resulting in difficulty cutting and coloring in a preschool setting. He quickly lost interest in activities that he could not compete successfully. When tasks were adjusted to his skill level, his willingness to engage increased. His lack of interest was related more to a mismatch between his skills and the task requirements than an attention problem.

A good clinician must look at the root cause of the behaviors and rule out other conditions. This is complicated when more than one disorder is present. Research suggests that up to 45% of children with ADHD have at least one other psychiatric disorder such as Oppositional Defiant Disorder, bipolar disorder, anxiety, or an emerging Pervasive Developmental Disorder.

Donald was not following teacher directions and insisted on doing what he chose to do in the classroom. He was aggressive, had frequent outbursts and temper tantrums, and seemed to delight in antagonizing others. Teachers felt that he was the happiest when in the midst of a fight or argument. After a thorough investigation, Donald was determined to have Oppositional Defiant Disorder (ODD) in addition to ADHD.

The root of any behavior must be looked at carefully and thoroughly. A neuropsychological evaluation by a developmental pediatrician may be necessary to rule out conditions whose symptoms might overlap with ADHD.

Joey had language delays and difficulty in processing auditory information. His preschool teachers complained that he did not follow directions but roamed around from place to place in his preschool classroom rather than working on the assigned task. A thorough language evaluation revealed that Joey did not process or understand many of the directions from his preschool teachers who gave only auditory directions. When auditory directions were paired with visuals, such as cue cards to remind him of expected behavior and a visual schedule to structure to his day, his rate of on-task behavior increased significantly.

In addition to developmental differences and symptom overlap with other conditions, life experiences and parenting styles can also cloud the picture. This doesn't mean that parenting causes ADHD. Rather, chaotic conditions can impact a child's behavior, causing him to have more disorganized behavior, mimicking ADHD. In addition to lack of a secure structured environment, studies have shown that the manner in which parents respond to a difficult child can impact the course of those behavior problems. A negative and critical style of management has been shown to predict the continuation of behavior problems into later years.

Preschool Issues

Preschools are very different settings from home and from most daycares. They have much more structure and more demands. Placing your son with ADHD in a preschool setting could bring additional stress to both you and your child. It is commonplace for children with ADHD who are oppositional or aggressive to be kicked out of daycares and preschools because of their disruptive behaviors. When talking to preschools, be honest about your son's behavioral difficulties to determine if they have had success in handling children like him.

Time spent researching the right fit between a preschool and your son could pay big dividends and enhance his self-esteem. You want to avoid early experiences of failure because of the stress they bring to you and your child. He is building his sense of self-esteem as a capable learner and participant in the educational setting from these early ages. Your choices may be limited according to your geographical location, but it will be important to find the best fit that you can.

Helpful Questions in Your Preschool Search

Philosophy. What is the school's mission statement and philosophy? Your goal is to find a school that seeks to understand a child's strengths and build from those rather than focusing on the negative. Preschool is only the beginning of a long educational experience, so having it begin in as positive a way as possible is critical. Some questions to consider might be:

◊ What are the teacher's expectations for what your son should be doing at his age? How do those expectations match his skill set?

◊ Are expectations the same for boys and girls? What accommodations do they make for boys? How adaptable is the program in accommodating individual needs? For example, if a child becomes too stimulated, is there a quiet space where the child can go and regroup but still be supervised?

◊ What rate of success has the school achieved in successfully engaging boys with ADHD? How parent-friendly is the school? Do they allow parent volunteers in the classroom? How do they communicate with parents and how often?

Physical set-up. Some questions to consider about the physical set-up of the preschool include:

◊ Is the environment inviting, colorful, warm, and comfortable?

◇ Is it well equipped with colorful materials to develop language skills, fine motor skills, early literacy, and math?

◇ What is the ratio of preschoolers to staff? Boys with ADHD function much better in small-group or individualized settings than in large-group activities.

Daily routine. Some questions to consider about the preschool schedule and routine include:

◇ Do children follow a structured schedule that is consistent?

◇ Does the teacher explain and model each desired behavior and practice until all students know exactly what is expected from them, including how to walk from place to place in line, sit in circle time, and raise a quiet hand to get the teacher's attention? (Some of these may be long-term goals.)

◇ Is movement throughout the day a key feature?

◇ How long are children expected to sit still?

Curriculum. Some questions to consider about the curriculum at the preschool include:

◇ Do they use theme-based units of study that focus on concepts (such as community helpers) as well as social skills? For example, the social skill of being a good friend could be taught through literature, songs, games, and role-playing.

◇ What kinds of continuing education do the teachers receive to enable them to keep up with trends and "what works" with children? For example, boys with ADHD typically do much better at the beginning of the school year, when things are new and fresh for them. They become easily bored, resulting in an increase of problem behaviors. A proactive preschool would be alert to those patterns and program activities to avoid boredom such as bringing in new, exciting educational materials periodically.

◇ Does the curriculum involve hands-on activities?

Behavior management. Some questions to consider about the preschool's behavior management style include:

◇ What are some techniques the teacher will use to gain and keep attention? Does she use frequent visual and verbal cues, maintain close proximity to active children so she can intervene quickly, and provide frequent feedback (Rief, 2008)? Does she try to hone in on what might be effective for individual children? For example, if your son can't sit still in circle time, could he be given an instrument to play while classmates are singing or a job to do, such as assisting the teacher, to redirect his attention in a positive way?

◇ What are their disciplinary techniques? How is time-out used and how often? If time-out does not prove effective for your son, what alternatives will be considered? Remember, if you son is placed in time-out often, he will miss learning opportunities.

◇ How closely are children monitored for safety?

Importance of Structure

As in the home setting, consistency and structure are critical for your son's success. It is important for him to be very clear about expectations and boundaries for his behavior, consequences, and rewards. The preschool structure should allow for the teaching of good school-related habits such as staying in an assigned space, following a routine, organizing a workspace, following teacher directions, cooperating with classmates, waiting for a turn, and cleaning up after completing a task.

Jim's son Teddy started out attending a Montessori preschool. Things seemed to go pretty well for about 3 months, and then the teachers started having conferences because Teddy was often "wandering about." He would go from area to area but not really complete any of the lessons, thus interfering with the other children's work. Jim and his wife decided that the Montessori program was not structured enough so they moved Teddy to a preschool with a traditional schedule. This helped because the class's daily schedule was more structured with a series of short activities, as compared to the more open schedule of the Montessori school.

As in the home setting, consistency and structure are critical for your son's success. It is important for you to be very clear about expectations and boundaries for his behavior, consequences, and rewards. Jim and his wife, Peggy, structured their home routine to help Teddy when he was a preschooler, using a behavior and reward chart that had a place to write the expected behaviors and a spot to place either a happy, sad, or neutral face if Teddy followed the behaviors. They explained the chart to him and reviewed it daily. For example, one rule was, "No screaming at Mom or Dad." Each day Teddy could earn a reward if he had a certain number of happy faces. This was a concrete way to teach Teddy responsibility and help him learn about the importance of self-control.

Teacher Characteristics

A preschool teacher who is firm but loving is important for your son. Energy and creativity are important, as well as a love of children and knowledge of their developmental differences. A teacher who is highly organized, is intuitive about behavior, and has situational awareness will assist a boy with ADHD in acclimating to his new situation. It will be important for the teacher to be effective in communicating concerns and positive accomplishments with you so you can work together as a team.

When Jim's son Teddy was in preschool, he was an active boy and enjoyed playing outside. One day during playground time, Teddy decided it would be fun to climb over the chain link fence that bordered the playground. Teddy made it to the top of the fence, and his teacher spotted him just as he was perched on the top with one foot dangling on either side of the fence. She calmly coached him down and helped him understand the importance of staying with the others. Teddy's teacher foiled his getaway plan but used it as a teaching opportunity to help him understand the importance of staying with the class.

Think back to the questions you can ask when finding a preschool for your son. You should directly talk to your son's potential teacher so you can get a feel for her personality. You don't want a teacher whose personality is totally soft spoken and flat, because your son can take advantage of her. On the other hand, you don't want a teacher who is gruff and intolerant. It's best to try to observe the teacher in action even if it means scheduling a time to return another day.

Considering Retention

Sometimes preschool staff may recommend having a boy repeat a year of preschool. Before that decision is made, there are many factors to consider. These include birth date, physical size, social maturity, fine motor skills, and progress in his current setting. Many parents of boys who have August or September birthdays decide that holding them back and having them repeat a year of preschool before entering kindergarten allows them to mature and be more ready for the academics presented in kindergarten. The important consideration is to try to determine if an additional year would make a significant difference in his performance. Try to project ahead and think about how this retention would impact him as an elementary school student, a teenager, and a college student.

If you are still not sure, take your son to a local school psychologist and have some educational testing done. For an investment of a few hundred dollars or less, a good psychologist can help you determine your son's readiness for elementary school. Many parents will invest in testing, considering that it is going to affect their child for the rest of his life. When we test preschool students for readiness, we often use the Wechsler Preschool and Primary

Scale of Intelligence, a preschool-age IQ test, and school readiness, tests such as the Woodcock-Johnson III Tests of Achievement or Kaufman Test of Educational Achievement. With each year that passes, it becomes harder to retain a student. Our advice is that if you are in doubt, then get it checked out.

When More Support Is Needed

As a parent, it is easy to be in denial about problems and postpone action. Monitor your son's behavior and adjustment carefully. Early intervention services can be very valuable to your child, so you will want to keep your eyes open to his needs. You don't want him to go for years with untreated symptoms that may cause difficulty with learning and social relationships and result in low self-esteem.

When more support is needed, you should consider a preschool designed to handle developmental delays that interfere with a child's functioning in a typical preschool environment. These delays would cover a wide array of conditions, including behavioral, speech and language, gross and fine motor, and intellectual delays. These preschools are usually offered in conjunction with community agencies and the public school. Federal law requires that school districts provide early identification and intervention services for children with disabilities whose deficits are severe enough to impact their functioning. If you think that your child's symptoms are severe enough, contact your local school district to find out how to access an evaluation and possible specialized preschool services. There will usually be a screening evaluation and then a more in-depth evaluation (if needed) to determine if your son qualifies for these services. Infants and toddlers may qualify for Part H services, and preschoolers (ages 3–5) may qualify for Part B services through the Individuals with Disabilities Education

Improvement Act (IDEA). See Chapter 6 for more discussion of legislation governing disabilities.

Chad's parents were at their wit's end because he had been asked to leave two daycare centers. Complaints from preschool teachers included throwing tantrums, hitting other children, throwing classroom tools, and refusing to stay in his assigned area. His parents had tried reasoning with, rewarding, and punishing him—all to no avail. After a thorough evaluation, including a cognitive assessment by a school psychologist, an in-depth speech-language evaluation by a speech language pathologist, an occupational therapy assessment, and a developmental history, Chad was determined to be eligible for a special needs preschool program that focused on behavioral goals along with emerging academic skills. The classroom had a low pupil-to-teacher ratio, additional assistance from a classroom aide, and a highly structured behavioral management program where behaviors were taught and reinforced. In addition, he had occupational therapy to help him improve his deficient fine motor skills that were impacting his ability to hold a pencil, cut, and color. Chad had his ups and downs but eventually improved in his ability to follow directions, stay in his assigned area, and keep his hands and objects to himself. Without that early intervention, Chad would have encountered much more difficulty in elementary school.

As noted previously, an evaluation by a developmental-behavioral pediatrician, neurologist, psychiatrist, school psychologist, clinical psychologist, or neuropsychologist might provide instructive information and give you more direction. For example, if a child was determined to have fine motor delays or sensory issues that impacted his performance, then occupational therapy might ameliorate some of his difficulties. If he had delays in pragmatic or social language that impacted his social skills, then language therapy and social skills groups might provide much-needed assistance.

Some school psychologists and clinical or neuropsychologists use an evaluation tool called a Developmental Neuropsychological

Assessment (NEPSY) to help diagnose ADHD in preschool-age boys. It is a test that measures your child's neurological development. This assessment can be used with preschool-age children, and it contains tests of attention. If your child's pediatrician recommends you try medication but you want a second opinion, find a psychologist who uses the NEPSY. If your preschool-age child really has ADHD, it should show up in the NEPSY test scores, providing a quantitative measure in diagnosing ADHD in preschool-age children. It also removes some of the subjectivity of parent and teacher rating forms.

Thus, if the preschool boy's NEPSY attention scores are average and at expected levels, then ADHD may not be present. Even if the parent and teacher rating forms scores are high for observing ADHD behaviors, it may be more of a behavioral issue than a true attention issue. Because most consider ADHD to be a neurological disorder, we would argue that a true ADHD disorder would have showed up in the neuropsychological testing scores. Thus, we would use the average neuropsychological test scores as the basis to recommend behavior therapy as a first intervention before recommending medication.

Medical Intervention With Young Boys

The challenges of managing a young boy in a structured, educational setting may prompt your son's preschool teacher to encourage you to try medication. The use of medication in young children with ADHD requires careful consideration of the severity of the behavior balanced with the side effects from medication. Most pediatricians recommend medication only when behavioral interventions implemented with fidelity over time have proven to be ineffective or when the child is exhibiting dangerous behavior. There are uncertainties over the long-term effects of medication on children's developing neurological structures. There are significantly fewer studies on preschool children than on older children.

As reported in the *Brown University Child and Adolescent Behavior Letter* ("Pharmacological . . . ," 2009), a review of four decades of research showed "that methylphenidate (Ritalin) has a greater evidence base than other medications, psychosocial interventions, and alternative treatments in the short-term treatment of ADHD in preschoolers" (p. 4). A National Institute of Mental Health study (Wolraich, 2007) found that the effectiveness of methylphenidate was more limited in preschoolers than in older children. Other studies have shown that preschool children can be more sensitive to side effects of medication, including irritability, insomnia, and weight loss (Bower, 2006).

However, the Food and Drug Administration (FDA) only recommends amphetamines (e.g., Adderall, Dexedrine, Vyvanse) for children as young as 3, according to Dr. Mark Wolraich (2007), professor of pediatrics at the University of Oklahoma. It is widely believed that the difference in the FDA recommendations for amphetamines versus methylphenidate "has more to do with the regulations that were in place when the FDA approved the medications than they do with how much evidence there is about how well amphetamines work or how safe they are in preschool-aged children" (Wolraich, 2007, para. 3). As cited in the *Brown University Child and Adolescent Behavior Letter*, doctors "have to balance exposing children's rapidly developing brains to psychopharmacological agents against the potentially damaging consequences of not treating the disorder" ("Pharmacological . . .", 2009, para. 3). It is very clear that if medication is used, then it should be closely monitored by medical personnel.

A review of the literature indicates fewer studies on the effects of various treatment approaches for ADHD in young children compared to older children. There are even fewer studies comparing the effectiveness of alternative treatments to pharmacological treatments. Alternative treatments include specific diets; supplements, especially herbal; biofeedback; parent training; and behavior therapies.

Some studies indicate that elimination diets (e.g., additive-free, sugar-free, carbohydrate-free) have shown some promising evidence. Some clinicians believe that diets higher in protein and lower in carbohydrates and sugars provide a more stable sugar level and prevent meltdowns based on metabolic problems, which might exacerbate ADHD.

A study of 135 preschoolers over a 5-year period released in 2007 and published in the *School Psychology Review* indicated that preschoolers with ADHD may require "more behavior therapies and less medication" (as cited in Breaden, 2007, p. 5). The September 2007 issue of the *Harvard Mental Health Letter* (Harvard Health Publications) suggested that "parent training and specialized day care should be considered before resorting to stimulant medication" (p. 1).

Home/Community Issues: Being a Proactive Parent

You know your child better than anyone else. Educate yourself to have a thorough understanding of ADHD and how your child's daily interactions are affected. The diagnostic criteria are the same for young children as for older children. If your child is diagnosed with ADHD as a preschooler, you will want to get him reevaluated when he enters school. Observe your child's presentation of the following characteristics of ADHD at home and determine ways you can assist him with:

◊   excessive activity,
◊   poor attention to tasks,
◊   impaired impulse control and ability to delay gratification,
◊   deficits in memory or storing information to use in guiding behavior in the future,
◊   difficulties with regulating emotions and motivation,
◊   diminished problem-solving ability,

◊ delayed developmental of internal language, and

◊ greater variability in quality of work.

Be a detective in determining ways your son's characteristics affect his daily functioning and try to provide supports when you can to help him work around and grow in his deficit areas. At all times, remember that some behaviors are not within your son's control. Everyone knows ADHD can carry long-term risks. As a proactive and informed parent, you will want to intervene as early as possible. Dr. Russell Barkley (2007) stated that even though ADHD is not *caused* by "how parents raise a child, how parents *respond* to and *manage* a child may contribute to the persistence of ADHD" (p. 86). He indicated that parents can make the problem better or worse by their response to the child.

Whether you son has been diagnosed or is suspected of having ADHD, there are a number of things you can do to help manage his behaviors in the home and community.

Engineering Success

Understand the Symptoms of ADHD

Knowledge can be a very powerful ally. A few things we recommend you do to learn more about ADHD include:

◊ Seek out parent training in effective management and discipline. Contact your pediatrician, community agencies, or school district for information. Behavior modification techniques, including immediate consequences, praise, ignoring negative behavior that is not dangerous, and teaching replacement behaviors, can be very effective.

◊ Learn what management tools are effective with your child. Distraction is often effective if you see your son starting to get upset.

◇ Be positive and focus on strength areas. If your son is innovative, provide items that will encourage that talent. If he enjoys helping others, try to engineer those opportunities. Try to praise your son several times a day for things he is doing correctly.

◇ Create an environment that promotes success. If your son is accident prone, put away items that can be easily broken. If he has trouble cleaning up toys, provide an organizational structure. Placing pictures on shelves or drawers can help in cleanup. If he has trouble transitioning from one activity to another, use a kitchen timer to count down the time before he has to switch activities, or give verbal warnings.

Structuring His Day

◇ Provide a structured environment with adequate opportunities for activity and rest. Meal times, naptime, and bedtime should be consistent. Some children benefit from having a visual schedule that shows their daily routine or a visual cue card to prompt certain behaviors.

◇ Prepare your son in advance when a change in schedule is unavoidable.

◇ Provide plenty of time for physical release throughout the day, including playing outside or engaging in some energy-releasing activity.

◇ Keep your son busy in productive activities. Idle time may create problems. Limit television and video game time and avoid those with violence. The American Academy of Pediatrics (n.d.) suggested that children younger than 2 years old should not watch entertainment on screens such as TV, DVDs, computers, video games, or videotapes. Limit television and video game time to no more than 2 hours a day in older children.

◇ Plan ahead for times when long periods of sitting will be required, such as when traveling in a car. Bring snacks, games, books, and videos (if he is older than 2) to keep him occupied.

◇ Be prepared to remove your son from highly stimulating activities if he becomes easily overwhelmed. Children frequently need some quiet time.

Managing Behaviors

◇ Make sure you know what behavior you expect of your son in different situations. Discussing expected behavior beforehand is often helpful.

◇ Practice how you would like to respond in situations to avoid overreacting.

◇ Be as consistent as possible. It is always important to muster the energy to follow through on directions and consequences. If not, you will likely pay for it later. Consistency enables your son to know exactly what you expect and to be clear about the rules. Behavior cues used consistently by parents and caregivers, as well as by teachers, can be critical.

◇ Monitor your son's activities closely for safety if he is impulsive. Cover electrical outlets and lock up cleaning products and other dangerous items. If your son is a climber who enjoys getting into kitchen cabinets, provide a cabinet at floor level just for him that contains items of interest.

◇ Some behavioral problems can be avoided by providing distractions if you see that your child is getting upset. Suggest a walk or sing a song (Alexander-Roberts, 2006).

◇ Use time out judiciously. Some experts estimate that time out should include 1 minute for each year up to 5 years of age. Time out can often begin at 2 years of age (Alexander-Roberts, 2006).

Teaching and Learning

◊ Keep eye contact with your son, especially when giving directions. If necessary, gently hold his chin so he is looking right at you to ensure he is listening. (Caveat: Be alert to situations where holding his chin could set up a power struggle. Sometimes it is better to avoid eye contact in dicey situations so as not to challenge or antagonize.)

◊ Keep directions clear and simple. Boys with ADHD are especially unreceptive to long directions or conversations. Keep directions to only one step until you are sure your child can handle two-step directions

◊ Provide repeated practice for new skills, especially social skills like sharing a toy. Children with ADHD seem to learn through experience and practice rather than by observing social cues.

◊ Don't assume that your son understands cause and effect. Specific training in identifying cause and effect relationships in stories, movies, and real-life situations can be helpful.

◊ Ensure that the environment is free from distracting stimuli when engaging in a teaching activity. Boys with ADHD are less able to screen out competing stimuli than other children.

◊ Allow fidget toys or items that may help the child sit and focus—for instance, when a book is read. Fidget items are things that keep the child's hands busy and serve to calm him. These can be favorite toys such as small cars, a stuffed animal, or a squishy, sensory toy. Websites such as http://www.addiss.co.uk are good sources of fidget toys.

◊ Use as many senses as possible when teaching a new skill. For example, when teaching the names of fruits, allow your son to draw them, touch them, smell them, and taste them. Interactive learning will be the most productive.

◊ Give him a head start on learning to focus and develop some internal limits on behavior. A kitchen timer or Time Timer (http://www.timetimer.com) can be used to help your son extend the time he can focus on one activity.

Support for Parents

There is no question that parents of boys with ADHD are under much more stress than parents of boys without ADHD. Mothers of boys with ADHD generally report more self-blame, social isolation, and lower levels of self-esteem about their parenting skills than other parents (Barkley, 2007). If you have more than one child with ADHD, then of course your stress level will be even more elevated. Your son's behavior is baffling and often disruptive to the entire family. You may feel you are constantly on guard and never have time to yourself. Even finding a babysitter who can handle your son effectively may be difficult.

Realize that time away from your son is important to allow you to regroup and keep a positive attitude. The search for a competent babysitter who understands your son will be well worth it. Find someone who is willing to be educated about his condition. Oftentimes, your son will respond more positively to someone who is willing to engage in high-energy activities while keeping in mind the importance of safety. If money limits your ability to have a babysitter, try to exchange babysitting duties with another parent who understands ADHD and its management techniques. You want to avoid putting your son in situations that could be damaging to his self-esteem.

Remember that you are human and will lose your patience from time to time. Build in little breaks that will make this less likely to happen. Finding a parent support group may be helpful if that group is positive and focused on sharing what works and new techniques and trends. A support group of parents of children who have ADHD can be aware of and share information on local resources and services. To find support groups, check the Internet, local colleges or school systems, or pediatricians or other health professionals. CHADD, an organization for children and adults with ADHD (http://www.chadd.org), may be available in your area.

Parent training specific to ADHD children is available through CHADD-sponsored Parent to Parent programs. More intense and specialized training, such as Parent Child Interaction Training, may be available in your community. Keeping up with the latest research can be helpful. Type "childhood ADHD" or "ADHD in preschool" into an Internet search engine to find the latest research findings.

Assistance With Siblings

In addition to the challenges in preschool and in the community, your son with ADHD will, of course, bring his difficulties into the home. His high activity level, impulsivity, and difficulty in organizing his own behavior will inevitably create conflict with siblings. Brothers and sisters are often jealous of the additional time parents must spend with a child with ADHD. They may actually see the child with ADHD as lucky and envy him. You must walk a fine line in helping other family members have some understanding of ADHD behavior while still treating the child as a full and integral member of the family.

We often recommend books to help parents explain ADHD to siblings. Books often allow for an open discussion within a supportive context and for children to identify with the issue or character. We recommend these three books: *My Brother's a World Class Pain: A Sibling's Guide to ADHD/Hyperactivity*; *Learning to Slow*

Down and Pay Attention: A Book for Kids About ADHD; and *Cory Stories: A Kid's Book About Living With ADHD*.

Don't be afraid to use the help of a professional psychologist or counselor to learn problem-solving approaches. The same parenting style that works for one child does not always work for another. Jim and his wife took two parenting classes that were offered at a local preschool. One class was called Conscious Discipline, and the other was Redirecting Children's Behavior. In one class, Jim learned a strategy to help him not to overreact to his son's behavior—STAR, or taking time to Stop, Take a deep breath, And Relax. Jim placed paper stars at strategic places around the house to give himself and his wife a visual reminder not to overreact.

Utilizing problem-solving approaches to difficulties can often result in positive resolutions to many problems. Family and behavioral therapy can often be helpful in establishing a cohesive family bond. Remember that it is often very difficult for a boy with ADHD to hold his behavior together in school and community settings. His behavior may disintegrate in the home setting, where he feels safe. Providing a quiet place where he can regroup without trampling on the rights of other family members will be important.

In our private practices, we teach parents to physically get on their son's level when they are talking to him. When standing, parents tower above their son. When talking to, disciplining, or teaching him, parents should kneel, sit, or bend down to look him in the eye. This simple technique has an amazing effect in getting active boys to actually listen and understand.

A second technique we teach parents and siblings of energetic and emotional boys is to lower one's voice as the boy's voice gets louder. Energetic preschool boys are often loud with their play and voices. An often-effective strategy is to talk softer and get down to a whisper as your son gets louder. Inevitably, your son will take your cue and start to whisper too.

A third strategy that often works well for preschool-age active boys is teaching parents and siblings to make a game of things.

Boys usually enjoy games, and their competitive nature fits well with playing racing games. For example, when cleaning up toys, Mary Anne would often race her son to see who could pick up the highest number of blocks the fastest. Because Teddy didn't always want to walk next to us, Emily, his sister, often played the game of follow the leader to get him where she wanted to go.

Self-Esteem

Self-esteem is a collection of beliefs a person has about himself. It begins developing in toddlerhood and continues throughout life. It fluctuates, because it is often based on interactions with others and opportunities for success. It can be defined as pride in one's self or self-respect.

Self-esteem in preschoolers is in its early, developmental stages. The preschool boy with ADHD has likely heard hundreds, if not thousands, of redirections from his parents, teachers, caregivers, and classmates. He is likely bombarded with many more negative than positive comments. All of these redirections and negative comments can take a toll on your young son's self-esteem.

Preschool-age boys with low self-esteem may say things like "I'm a bad boy" or "Stop it, me. Be quiet." They may hear this from their classmates and even some teachers and parents. You may even overhear your young son say these things when he is angry or frustrated at himself. If your son says negative comments about himself, give him a hug and reassure him that you love him just the way he is. You can admit that his behavior sometimes frustrates you but that you still love him very much. Tell him that there is nothing he can do to make you stop loving him. Each night when you tuck him into bed, make it a nightly ritual to tell him how much you love him.

Strategies to Increase Self-Esteem

Helping your son develop a "can-do" attitude must be based on opportunities to accomplish realistic tasks. Don't expect more from him than he is capable of giving. His frustration tolerance may be limited, so patience will be required.

Giving honest, accurate feedback will help him as he develops his view of himself. Do not compare him to other children, especially siblings. More than likely, he will be making his own comparisons.

Providing a safe, secure environment for him, both at home and at school, will enable him to be able to take risks as he strives to accomplish tasks. Give him chances to make some of his own decisions and help him learn to solve problems.

Most preschool-age boys with ADHD love it when adults read out loud to them. Books are a great resource to help build the self-esteem of preschool boys. A few books we recommend to our clients with preschool-age boys include *No David!*; *Alexander and the Terrible, Horrible, No Good, Very Bad Day*; *I'm Gonna Like Me: Letting Off a Little Self-Esteem*; and *Love You Forever*. Reading books like these with your son helps him identify with the character, learn how the character solves a problem or learns a new behavior, and then apply that solution to his life. Books provide a nonthreatening and peaceful way to teach your child and build his self-esteem.

Begin by asking your son to sit on your lap or right next to you so you can both see the pictures. As you read the book aloud, use an animated voice. Help your son identify with the character by pointing out similarities between him and the character. Look for positive things that are related to the character and your son in addition to troublesome behaviors.

For example, in *No, David!* by David Shannon, the character likes chicken but forgets to chew with his mouth closed at the dinner table. If this happens to your son, mention that the boy in the book forgets to chew with his mouth closed too and look at what his mom says. Discuss how you tell your son to chew with his mouth closed, and then mention that it's an important manner to learn. At the end of the book, reinforce how much David's mom loves him and how much you love your son too. Most boys enjoy having the same book read to them multiple times, so each time you reread the book, you should emphasize different points to help your son.

There are additional activities you and your preschool son can do to help build self-esteem. One way is to provide your young son with an age-appropriate journal. One of our colleagues, Dr. Janet Mentore Lee, wrote a kid's journal called *The Daily Doodle: A Journal for Children Ages 4–7*. Dr. Lee describes her journal as a way to help kids feel reassured, validated, and supported. Each page of the activity book is a writing, scribbling, or doodling prompt that will help your child express his inner thoughts, feelings, and coping skills. Depending on his developmental level, you can help him write words or letters. *The Daily Doodle* provides prompts and is a great way to collaborate, create, and connect with your child, critical components to a parent-child relationship and building self-esteem.

Another activity you can do with your preschool son is to help him create a self-portrait. A large piece of butcher paper or many copy-sized sheets of paper taped together work well. Place the paper on the floor and ask your son to lie on top of it. Use a pencil or marker and then trace the outline of his body. Tell him you'd like to work with him to make a self-portrait. Use his and your favorite art supplies, which could include crayons, paint, ink, chalk, and so forth. Place a small mirror within reach and encourage him to look at it frequently. Help him by drawing in his ears, eyes, and mouth, and allow him to color his features. Comment about his beautifully colored eyes, nice hair, wide smile, or strong arms. When the project is completed, hang it up in his room. You could even take his picture next to it and tell him you are going to e-mail it to relatives, share it with friends, and brag about how cool he and his portrait look. An alternative to the life-size portrait is just to draw the shape of your son's head on paper and then allow him to color in his facial features.

Regardless of the activity you complete with your son, it's important to reinforce how much you love him and enjoy being with him. Try not to stress too much if he is wiggly while you read or squirms as you trace his outline. You have to keep the mindset of having fun and reinforcing his positive qualities. As a parent of a preschooler with ADHD, Jim always tried to strive for a ratio of five positive comments to one negative comment, but he rarely achieved it. To encourage himself he even bought a small counter to keep in his hand and click as he said positive comments. This helped for a while as he tried to change his mindset toward saying more positive comments.

Points to Consider

1. It is important to remember that organization, thinking before acting, and being able to sustain attention are all developmental by nature, meaning that behaviors can occur within a range of ages and still be considered within the normal range.

2. Time spent in researching the right fit between a preschool and your son could pay big dividends and enhance his self-esteem.

3. As a parent, it is easy to be in denial about problems and postpone action. Be proactive.

4. You will walk a fine line in helping other family members have some understanding of ADHD behavior while treating the child as a full and integral member of the family.

Action Steps to Take Now

1. Develop a stronger relationship with your son's preschool and ensure that his needs are being addressed. Use the questions in this chapter if you interview prospective preschools for your son.

2. Be a detective in determining ways your son's characteristics affect his daily functioning, and try to provide supports when you can to help him work around and grow in his deficit areas.

3. Recognize your child's temperament or pattern of personality characteristics. Structure his environment to enhance chances of good behavior.

4. Seek out parent training in effective management and discipline.

5. Try some of the tools we suggest in this chapter such as using books, becoming a STAR, changing tasks into games, or getting down to his level when you talk.

6. Be positive and focus on your child's strengths.

Chapter 4

The Elementary Years

Most ADHD diagnoses come during a child's elementary school years. So if you've skipped Chapters 1, 2, and 3 and turned directly to this page, you wouldn't be alone. (We just hope that when things settle down—as much as they ever do with an elementary-aged son with ADHD—you'll start again from the beginning.)

Here's what's happening: Your son's emotions are still developing, but he's way behind the curve of other kids his age. He may look like a little man, but he's really a bundle of raw emotions and feelings strung together in an almost primal way. You need to spend extra time teaching him how to stop and think, rather than just react because it will not come naturally to him. And you'll need a ton of patience, because those times you'll need to do the teaching will be exactly the times you'll be most challenged by his behavior.

Your son is in school full-time now, and he'll likely be expected to master the same curriculum as all of the students around him.

Both of you will need plenty of tools to meet this goal without lowering the bar for his academic success, and we'll spend a lot of time in this chapter sharing strategies that will help your son succeed in the classroom. Your son's teachers will be a critical part of his success, and we'll help you identify some of the characteristics of school settings where a boy with ADHD can flourish.

These are the years when your son is learning basic skills and work habits he'll use for the rest of his life. We're not going to sugarcoat it—these years can be tough. But there is tremendous satisfaction in knowing that all of the hard work, patience, and consistency you invest now will establish a firm foundation for your son.

We've been in the trenches, and we know that sometimes it seems like the struggles are never going to end. But take our word for it. One day, you're going to look back and say, "Wow, those years went by fast."

Going to School

Your son's elementary school career will be full of ups and downs. Each year, he will face new challenges and expectations. His behavior and adjustment to school will be related to how well he can handle the increased demands on his organizational skills and coping mechanisms. For most students, ADHD impacts not only their focus but also their ability to inhibit behavior and their executive functioning skills (e.g., planning, remembering, organizing). If your child responds impulsively, he does not have the luxury of planning ahead, thinking about what hc has learned in the past, or delaying gratification (Barkley, 2000a). As boys move from preschool to elementary school, they will be called upon to be more independent, organized, and goal-directed—areas that are weaknesses for most boys with ADHD. Barkley (2000a) stated, "The solution . . . is not to carp at those with ADHD to simply try harder," but to provide ". . . the sorts of cues, prompts, physical reminders and other captivating information that will guide behavior toward the intended goal" (p. 33).

One mother told us her son, Lionel, was a mess. His teacher told her Lionel always had papers everywhere—shoved and crumpled ones in his desk, several scattered on the floor around his desk, and others pouring out of folders where they had been hastily shoved. None of the children wanted to sit at his table because he was always bothering them to ask what he should do next. Furthermore, the class received rewards based on their table's performance, and all of the children knew Lionel would lose points for his table. His inability to be accepted by his classmates didn't stop there. At recess, none of the children wanted to play with Lionel because he was so rough and often hurt them, even though he always apologized without being prompted and said he didn't mean to hurt anyone.

Academically, Lionel was falling behind in all subjects, especially reading comprehension and math problem solving—two of the areas that required the most concentration and memory. His parents didn't know how to help him when he got home, because they could not read the scribble in his agenda planner, and Lionel never knew what he was supposed to do. They actually dreaded picking him up from school, because he often had meltdowns in the car based on how his school day had gone. He would cry because none of his classmates picked him for their team. Lionel often said the very words that tear at a parent's heart: "Everybody hates me!" The saddest part was that they knew he was not exaggerating, because he was rarely invited to any birthday parties or to play at anyone's house. They had always known he wasn't the perfect, well-behaved child, but he had managed to fit in much better in kindergarten, first grade, and second grade than he had in third grade. It seemed that the other boys were maturing and leaving Lionel in the dust.

Problem-Solving Perspective Required

If you are like most parents of boys with ADHD, you will find that your son's elementary years will be filled with learning and new challenges for you as well. There will be little room for complacency. Just when you think you've figured out how to handle your son's difficulties and are experiencing a period of smooth sailing, a new problem will pop up. If an ADHD boy is anything during these years, we've found that he is consistently inconsistent. In talking about kids with ADHD, Dr. Sam Goldstein (2004) said, "They know what to do, but do not consistently, predictably, or for that matter, independently do what they know" (p. 1).

We recommend that you adopt this stance: Look at every situation that arises as simply another puzzle with a solution. You and your son will fare much better if you keep that problem-solving perspective, because you never know when you will need it. Even when challenges come at you fast and furious—and we know they will, especially during the elementary years—we encourage you not to feel defeated by problems as they arise. Don't let your son feel beaten either. Instead, make sure he knows that together you're going to look at your resources and your capabilities and work to make things better. As his world has gotten bigger, your team can also grow. You can turn to his teacher, his principal, his school guidance counselor or psychologist, his doctor, and trusted friends for help and support. Part of the problem-solving mentality is remembering that you don't have to have all of the answers yourself.

Elementary schools are not the same as when you were a student. Your son is faced with high-stakes testing, mandatory retention, curriculum that doesn't account for differing developmental levels, reduced opportunities for recess, and a complex social milieu. Don't despair. Some positive changes may actually make your son's life easier. Schools and teachers are much more knowledgeable about ADHD and how to effectively serve those students. Increased use of technology in the classroom is also a plus for most boys with ADHD.

When you factor in his ADHD and the likelihood that your son may also have academic deficits, he is definitely going to need your involvement and support if he is to develop and maintain a positive attitude toward learning. It is well-documented that children diagnosed with ADHD often have learning disabilities and lower performance on standardized testing. There will be increased demands on his organizational skills and persistence, often exceeding his capability. These are critical years for him when he is cementing his view of himself. Your goal will be to help him be as independent as possible while providing enough support to enable him to view himself as a capable learner. Educate yourself so you can make the best possible choices for him.

Emotional/Behavioral Developmental Milestones

Along the way, your son is maturing a little bit every day, albeit more slowly than children without ADHD. Boys with ADHD usually have great difficulty with regulating emotions and with self-control. To keep tabs on your son's progress, try to have some awareness of when these developments occur in the general population. Based on research and child development theory, consider the following stages of development (Teeter, 1998):

◊ Ages 6–9: Self-control improves and more internal thinking develops.

◊ Middle childhood: Children are influenced by and use standards set by parents.

◊ Ages 7 and up: Self-talk guides behavior and enables children to take the perspective of others.

◇ Ages 6–12: Children become more adept at regulating emotional reactions to situations.

◇ Ages 10–12: Children are better able to control negative feelings and separate actions from feelings.

Consider one boy, Juan, who was cruising along in kindergarten and first grade. He seemed to be able to hold it together during sedentary classroom time until recess, when teachers commented that he became a "wild man," totally different than he was in the classroom. At the end of first grade, his best friend (who also happened to be one of the most popular kids in the class) deserted him. Juan liked to direct what they would play, which had become tiresome for his friend. His ability or willingness to take the perspective of others had not yet developed. In second grade, Juan found himself without a best friend and in a class with a teacher who was very rigid, cold, and boring. Juan was advanced academically. When he completed his work before everyone else, his teacher made his sit silently and would not allow him to work on anything else. One day, while his mother was presenting a program on her job to Juan's class, she realized just how sad her son had become while at school. He had stopped participating in class and lost his spunk. Juan began to balk at going to school and became depressed. As is typical of a young boy with ADHD, Juan was having difficulty regulating his emotions. He often had to be carried to the car, kicking and screaming, because his mother knew that allowing him to miss school because of a tantrum would only make the problem worse. After many conferences and much insistence from his parents, the school transferred him to another second-grade classroom, where the teacher immediately recognized Juan's need for permissible movement, stimulating activities when he finished his work, and assistance in developing his social skills. Even though the change was positive, it took time for Juan to make the adjustment. His parents had to continue trying to provide opportunities to make social connections and to help him regain his interest in school. It finally happened but was years in the making.

School Choices

Your choice of schools (and whether you have a choice at all) will depend upon where you live, your financial situation, and whether your local school district allows freedom to move from one school to another. In some cases, your local public elementary school may be your one and only option. If that's your family's situation, we encourage you to keep reading; what you learn here may help your school become a more welcoming place for all children with ADHD, including your own son.

However, many communities offer a variety of choices—public schools, charter schools, and private schools. Some school districts have online schools in which students complete class work via the computer. Homeschooling is another option we discuss in Chapter 6.

It is critical that you select the type of environment that will provide the best learning opportunities for your son. Time spent researching your options will likely pay off and will certainly give you peace of mind that you did the best that you could.

Consider the overall philosophy of the school. Boys with ADHD do better in schools with structure, good communication with parents, solid curriculum that matches instruction to the child's abilities, energetic teachers who utilize experiential learning and a variety of instructional techniques, high expectations for learners, and reasonable class sizes. It is important for the staff to have an understanding of ADHD as a neurobiological condition with deficits in impulse control and executive functioning, so they don't immediately attribute a boy's problems to laziness and lack of motivation. When you're evaluating a school, we recommend you ask the following questions:

◊ Does the curriculum match state guidelines? In most states, you can go to your state department of education's website and access the curriculum for various grades.

◊ What is the average class size? Smaller is often better; 20 students or fewer is optimal.

◊ Does it appear to be a highly organized and structured environment?

◊ Do the students sit in desks or at tables? A highly distractible child usually does better at a desk.

◊ Does the school provide opportunities, such as tutoring, for extra help if a child lags behind academically?

◊ What kind of success rate has the school had for boys with ADHD?

◊ Is close supervision provided at all times, especially during transitions?

◊ What is the school's communication policy with parents?

◊ Is the school willing to accommodate his needs with strategies such as preferential seating, frequent cueing to task, or allowing movement as long as it does not disturb others?

◊ What is the behavior management plan? Is it proactive and designed to eliminate opportunities for misbehavior? Children with ADHD benefit from positive reinforcement, contingency management, and being held accountable for their behavior.

◊ Does the staff make organization a priority and assist students in developing organization skills?

Teacher/Classroom Match Is Important

Once you have selected a school, a good plan of action may be to have a conversation with the principal and provide some information about your son to help the school make a good teacher match for him. Some teachers are much more effective than others in dealing with boys with ADHD. The ultimate decision will be up to the principal, who has to consider many factors. Teachers who are patient, have high energy, and are structured and loving but firm are usually most effective with boys with ADHD. One confounding factor about these children is that their focus is often governed by their motivation, so it is key to have a teacher who tries to make learning interesting. Some families have the good fortune to find a teacher who is flexible enough to work with their son's built-in restlessness. Those teachers allow children to move about after tasks are complete, as long as it does not bother other students. Or they might allow a boy to stand beside his desk and work. Having a teacher who can appreciate your son for his strengths and not become too annoyed with his impulsivity and activity level will be invaluable.

Information for Your Teammates: Your Son's Teachers

The quality of your young son's education can have a direct relationship to his adult life. In our practices, we have observed excellent teachers who know exactly what strategies work with boys with ADHD. As your son's most powerful advocate, you should have a solid understanding of instructional techniques that might help your son and share them with his teachers. More than likely, many of his teachers will already be implementing many of these strategies. You can develop your own personalized list of interventions that seem to help your son and share them with new teachers when appropriate. Your goal is always to establish a collaborative relationship, not to tell the teacher how to run his or her classroom. You might even want to incorporate some of these techniques during homework time.

Classroom Organization/Management

In an ideal world, your son's educational environment will include:

◊ a positive classroom environment where the teacher has an understanding of ADHD and is familiar with strategies to prompt your son to become an active participant in the learning process;

◊ specific classroom procedures established and practiced consistently. In kindergarten, children may need practice to understand how to stand in line, take turns, raise their hands, and wait to be called on before speaking;

◊ organizational skills taught and modeled throughout the school day, with assistance where necessary. Use of color-coded folders for each subject and a separate folder for homework can be very helpful;

◊ seating in a distraction-free area, close to the point of instruction but as far away as possible from air conditioners, high-traffic areas, bathroom access, and other active students;

◊ provision of a study carrel or separate area of the classroom where a child can choose to go and work when distractions become too great. In some cases, students have referred to these areas as their offices;

◊ work areas that are kept neat and free of distractions;

◊ placement of students with ADHD near positive role models;

◊ when possible, core classes that are scheduled early in the day. An optimal schedule for a boy with ADHD is to have lunch and physical education or recess at intervals that break up the day;

◊ achievement motivators that stress effort and persistence. In other words, the child is rewarded for doing his very best, not for producing an "A" result;

◊ concept of time-out used as a chance to regain control rather than as a punishment;

◊ supervision, especially during transition times. Boys with ADHD are more likely to get in trouble while moving from one area to another;

◊ allowance for movement as long as other students aren't disturbed. For example, the boy with ADHD may be allowed to get out of his desk to retrieve something, walk around the classroom, go to the restroom, or get a drink of water. Work by Rapport and others (2008) suggested that activity may serve a purpose in helping students with ADHD to process information; and

◊ acceptable substitutes for motor behavior such as allowing the student to squeeze stress balls or chew gum if permitted by the school.

Behavior: Rewards and Consequences

Children with ADHD may require more relevant rewards and consistent consequences for behavior than other children. An individualized behavior plan using tangible rewards is sometimes necessary and can be developed by the teacher, a school psychologist, or a behavior specialist. Stickers, happy faces, or check marks can be redeemed for opportunities for extra computer time, to mentor another student, to be a teacher's helper, or to have lunch with a special teacher or administrator. Sometimes a response/cost plan, whereby a student can also lose something for poor behavior, works for some students and may be necessary for serious behavior. For example, if a student hits someone, he might lose all of his points for the day or lose one of the privileges he had already earned. It is critical for rewards or consequences to be delivered as close to the behavior as possible. It's important to bear the following in mind as you implement this practice for boys with ADHD:

◇ Sincere verbal praise for specific behavior is invaluable as a tool for reinforcing the desired behavior. Make sure to "catch him being good."

◇ Students should be taught how to become independent learners and how to self-monitor their own behavior.

◇ Frequent visual cues between student and teacher help the boy maintain optimal attention and control his behavior. A cue could be a special sign that only the boy with ADHD and his teacher know. This is a great proactive way to help a child.

Lesson Presentation

Teaching boys with ADHD sometimes requires a little bit more ingenuity (and a lot more patience). Ask your son's teacher to think of this list as extra tools for his or her toolbox:

◇ Give directions in short sentences, accompanied with visuals when possible. In the upper elementary grades, it is often helpful for a child to see what the finished product should look like.

◇ Offer assistance breaking down longer assignments into manageable chunks. Some children are overwhelmed by the amount of information on a page and benefit from covering part of the page with a blank sheet of paper. When a child is overwhelmed, he often shuts down rather than attempting to start on a project.

◇ Establish eye contact with a child with ADHD before delivering key points of instruction. Watch for signs that indicate lack of comprehension, especially daydreaming.

◇ Provide frequent review and repetition of previously learned material.

◇ Understand the child's capability and provide lessons that are challenging without being frustrating.

◊ Hands-on, experiential learning is a favorite for boys with ADHD. Their attention to task increases significantly when it is of high interest.

◊ Ignore minor inappropriate behavior (Parker, 2005).

◊ Provide warnings before transitions (e.g., "Five more minutes before science").

◊ Demonstrate proper behavior. Helping a boy compensate for social skills deficits can be very beneficial, especially in younger grades. Sharing and turn-taking can be especially difficult for young children with ADHD. Teachers can model behavior, reinforce appropriate behavior, and help the child initiate interactions.

◊ Use of computerized instruction as part of the curriculum is a positive way for most boys with ADHD to learn, because it is stimulating and interactive.

◊ Target his learning style. Because boys with ADHD can be incredibly focused on topics or activities of their choice, an effective motivator can be to allow them extra credit on selected topics with the project to be matched to their learning style. If a boy is talented verbally, then he might research something and present to the class. If he's good with his hands, he might build a project instead.

Your Son's Peers

Outside of your family, your son's school offers the most important opportunities for his socialization, and elementary school is when your son should be making great strides in learning how to appropriately interact with others. During this time it is common for boys with ADHD to have one of two problems:

◊ They may lack social skills appropriate for their age.

◊ They may have the skills but may not stop and think before they act.

If your son is having problems with his peer group at school, it is important to know what is at the root of the problem. More than likely, his teacher can share information about his functioning in the classroom, and you can make observations on your own at birthday parties or other social outings.

Dr. John Taylor (2001), a clinical family psychologist, has classified children and adolescents with ADHD as having difficulty in many of the following areas:

◊ turn-taking in games and conversation,
◊ accepting criticism,
◊ losing in games or competitions,
◊ understanding and following instructions,
◊ honoring other people's "personal space,"
◊ resisting peer pressure, and
◊ disagreeing with others and solving problems.

If you have pinpointed some problem areas for your son in the above list, then you can go about helping him acquire those skills in a number of ways.

◊ Communicate with his teacher and solicit his or her help. Sometimes children need to be explicitly taught social skills; they don't acquire them by osmosis. Some schools have social groups run by a guidance counselor or school psychologist where children are taught skills and have the opportunity to practice them using role playing. Some classroom teachers are excellent at weaving social expectations into their daily curriculum and setting up opportunities where children can interact successfully.

◊ There are a number of books written for children that highlight social skills through the use of stories that you can read and discuss with your son. This notion is called bibliotherapy. One of Jim's previous books, *Teaching Problem Solving Through Children's Literature*, contains book titles and specific lesson plans for each book that teachers or parents can use to help kids increase their social skills.

◊ There are also games, such as *Do Watch Listen Say* by Quill, and interactive CDs, such as *My School Day Enhanced* and *You Are a Social Detective* by Social Skill Builder, Inc., that teach social skills interactively.

Consider one student we worked with, Quavon. He was a fifth grader who had previously been diagnosed with ADHD, Inattentive Type. He was very timid and did not know how to initiate interactions with his classmates. One day he complained to his teacher on the basketball court at recess that no one would play with him. She grabbed the ball and said, "Quavon, you and I will make a great team," and they began to play. Within 5 minutes, a number of other boys had joined the game. The fact that the teacher chose to play with Quavon elevated his status in his peers' eyes. The teacher continued to set up situations where Quavon could interact comfortably, and little by little, his skills began to grow. This was a great way to increase his social skills.

A Quick Look at Causes, Presentations, and Possible Solutions

As we have stressed throughout the book, no two boys with ADHD will be alike. Your son's ADHD may manifest itself in very different ways than another boy's. Scan the chart in Table 3 to see if you recognize any familiar behaviors. If you do, it will help you understand not only the likely causes but also ways you might work with your son to overcome the challenge.

One student, Cody, reached all of his developmental milestones early and appeared to be a very bright child in many ways. However, since early childhood, Cody had shown real difficulty

Table 3

Causes, Presentations, and Solutions for ADHD

Cause	Presentation	Possible Solutions
Faulty sense of time	• Always late and behind schedule • Doesn't get started on tasks • Misses deadlines • Doesn't start tasks promptly • Poor planning	• Use agenda or planner • Create a behavior plan • Break assignments down • Use prompts and reminders • Maintain a schedule
Impulsivity	• Acts before thinking • Doesn't consider consequences • Jumps from one task to another • Doesn't listen to others • Blurts out in class • Limited self-control	• Provide structure • Teach verbal rehearsal • Share stop/think strategies • Conduct role-playing
Inflexibility	• Trouble with transitions • Easily agitated • Uncooperative	• Give prior notice for transitions • Teach coping skills
Inattention	• Disorganized • Loses items • Unable to listen • Forgets task of moment • Doesn't store material in memory • Thinks of many things at once	• Teach self-monitoring • Create a designated place for items • Insist on eye contact • Use organization tools • Use memory strategies
Overarousal	• Fidgeting • Excessive talking • Constant movement • Easily stimulated	• Give student permissible movements • Use of fidget item • Provide calm areas • Ignore low-level behaviors

tearing himself away from things he enjoyed, especially outside play, play dates, computer or video games, and watching television. He was very unorganized. He was always forgetting something, and his backpack was a mess. No previous attempts at organization seemed to have helped. In spite of his disorganization, Cody sailed through school until third grade, where he was having some difficulty with reading comprehension and writing assignments. He'd never been an avid reader and never wanted to complete a book. When reading aloud, he omitted or incorrectly read words, which impacted his comprehension. He had difficulty summarizing a story and answering higher-order thinking questions about a story, especially if it was about a topic in which he had limited interest. His teachers noted inconsistency in his writing. Some of his writing was targeted and followed rules of grammar and punctuation, but other times it was full of run-together sentences and disorganized ramblings. Cody excelled in math and could solve multistep problems in his head. But he had difficulty with multiplication facts and showing his work on multistep problems.

Luckily for Cody, he was already in a structured, predictable classroom setting with an enthusiastic teacher who was determined to figure out strategies to help him be successful. She worked with his parents to establish weekly communication about his progress. His parents agreed to have Cody empty his backpack every night and get all of the papers in their proper places. They helped him establish a designated place by the door where he could put all of his school items for the next day. He earned video game time based on the number of minutes of independent reading he did. At school, Cody was motivated to use a monitoring checklist, developed by his teacher, which was broken down by subject. He was placed on a reward system and was able to select his reward from a menu of reinforcers that he could earn dependent on his total number of points, which included additional time on the computer, opportunities to assist his teacher, and homework passes. He was required to self-monitor on the items shown in Table 4 with teacher oversight.

In Mary Anne's work as a school psychologist in the public school system, individualized behavior and/or self-monitoring plans are often developed for students. Cody's plan had its ups and downs, but his teacher was able to establish that he did not have academic skill deficits but rather performance deficits. Everyone was motivated by his progress—his teacher, his parents, and most importantly, Cody. His situation shows that interventions in the classroom and at home are often multifaceted and require commitment from all involved parties, especially the child, in order to be successful.

Being a Proactive Parent/ General Home Interventions

Home plays a far more important role than just a place to do homework (which we'll cover in the next section). In fact, the expectations you set for your son at home are just as important to his success as anything that happens in his classroom.

In our practices we recommend that you extend the concepts of structure, activity, and discipline into your home. It's important that your son understand that school is not the only place he needs to maintain self-control, nor is it the only place where he can depend on a certain amount of structure and sameness. Some things to try include the following:

◊ Provide a structured home setting. Have a predictable schedule and try to stick to it.

◊ Try to avoid sending your son to school tired. He will have to expend so much energy to battle his ADHD during the day and will need some reserves.

◊ Help him establish some order in his room, especially for important things. He should have a specific place to keep

Table 4

Self-Monitoring Chart

All Subjects	Good (2)	Fair (1)	Needs Work (0)
Did I have all materials ready and available?			
Did I catch myself daydreaming and bring myself back to my work?			
Reading			
Did I use comprehension strategies when reading?			
Did I reread if the sentence did not make sense?			
Writing			
Did I complete a brief diagram to organize my writing?			
Did I proofread all of my writing for complete sentences, punctuation, and capitalization?			
Math			
Did I follow a plan my teacher gave me to solve math word problems?			
Bonus points for kind deeds, extra work, or exceptional behavior:			

his backpack, lunch box, or anything traveling with him daily to school.

◊ Until he naturally is able to keep order to his backpack, have him empty it every night and put all of the papers in their proper places.

◊ Provide a quiet, uncluttered homework center. Eliciting his help in selecting and creating the space might result in more compliant use.

◊ Try to feed him a healthy, balanced diet that is not loaded with processed food.

It's likely that your son with ADHD looks forward to recess or physical education because they allow him to blow off steam and release some of the excess energy that can build up. It's no different when he's at home, where you might try the following:

◊ Make sure that he has ample opportunity for activity. If he tends to be sedentary, don't give up until you find an active outlet that he enjoys. Some parents find that children benefit from running or riding their bike *before* going to school in the mornings.

◊ Make sure your son is not overscheduled so he has ample opportunity for breaks, activity, and sleep. You want to strive for a balance—enough activities for exposure but not an overload.

◊ Try to avoid placing him in situations where the problems associated with his ADHD will be aggravated. Think ahead.

Never presume that because your son is in school, it's now his teacher's responsibility to see that he behaves properly. That job is yours as well. We do recommend that you establish a system for communicating with his teacher (whether it is via e-mail, notes in the agenda planner, or on a daily behavior log), so you can work as a team to steadily improve your son's behavior and self-discipline. At home, try to put these practices in place:

◊ Work to understand the difference between willful acts of disobedience and behaviors that are the result of his ADHD and may not be under his control. Deal with them accordingly, because open defiance should have definite consequences. Impulsive behaviors may provide teachable moments where you can help your son develop strategies for dealing with his ADHD.

◇ Give directions in short, concise sentences, using prompts or visual reminders if memory seems to be an issue.

◇ Provide plenty of positive reinforcement and limit the negatives to the really important things. We definitely advise parents to pick their battles. Remember, your son probably gets plenty of negative feedback outside the home. There is a difference between being firm and being overly critical.

◇ Provide consequences within short order of the offending act. Providing them consistently is also key.

Homework

Be honest. You'd rather walk over hot coals than try to get your son to do his homework, wouldn't you? It's daunting for so many reasons. He probably had a frustrating day at school and doesn't look forward to sitting down at a desk again. Frequently boys with ADHD have weaker executive functioning skills and have great difficulty initiating activity, planning, and organizing. They honestly may not even remember what the teacher wants them to do. Mary Anne's son never liked to settle down to do homework and usually waited until the last minute. In high school, he always put off planning for large projects, especially term papers and science projects.

Jim's son's homework was, and is, a nightly battle. In Jim's experience, this is classic ADHD behavior. Homework requires sustained mental effort—and that's difficult for boys with ADHD. Over time Jim and his wife have found that applying Grandma's Rule works. Grandma's Rule means you have to eat your veggies before you can have dessert. In other words, work comes before play. Thus, Jim's son has to complete his homework before he can play any video games, one of his preferred activities. Teddy's 504 plan also includes a reduction in his homework load and receiving his homework early, so he can get started over the weekend. These accommodations help reduce frustrations.

Homework can be very stressful. The following guidelines have worked for our families:

◊ Establish ground rules and stick to them. For example, turn off the television and loud music, and don't permit your child to receive telephone calls or text messages during study time.

◊ Figure out the optimal time for homework in your household. Some children need a break after school, and others cannot be corralled after playing outside.

◊ Determine how long your son can work without becoming frustrated. Provide frequent activity breaks.

◊ Remember that he may have difficulty figuring out where to start and how to approach different tasks. Help him to learn to prioritize tasks so the most difficult and important ones are done first. Guide him in making a plan and taking one task at a time. You may need to cut assignments into parts so he doesn't feel overwhelmed.

◊ Provide help when needed, but do not become so involved that your son is not independent—a very fine and tricky balance.

◊ Allow him to use the computer or iPad (with teacher permission) for producing written work.

◊ If homework time produces too much conflict that cannot be resolved, then consider the services of a tutor (if you can afford it).

High-Stakes Testing

In most states, standardized testing plays a role in a school's evaluation and sometimes in whether a student is promoted. These tests are usually 45–90 minutes long, often have a great deal of information on a page, and can be very tedious and boring—clearly not optimal for boys with ADHD. Accountability is critical, so it is important to help your son make the best of the situation. Many school districts have practice tests on the computer, an effective way for a boy with ADHD to learn. Take advantage of opportunities for your son to practice if they are available.

Work to learn more about what is covered on the test and try to incorporate some of those skills into your daily interactions with your son. For example, if fractions are on the test, involve him in measuring when cooking or when building a project. If he might be asked to make a prediction about what he thinks may happen in a story, then ask him to make a prediction when you are watching a television program together.

From time to time, a boy with ADHD has heightened anxiety because he recognizes that he has performance deficits. Try to be sensitive to that possibility and help him figure out coping strategies to use when he is anxious such as breathing deeply or visualizing himself in a peaceful place. You and his teacher will walk a fine line between motivating him to do his best and putting too much pressure on him. If your son needs extended time or other accommodations related to his ADHD, a 504 plan or IEP can be considered (see Chapter 6).

Retention

Most studies have not shown benefits to retention. However, it is a decision that must be made based on individual circumstances, the educational environment, and advice from educators and others involved with your son. Some questions to ask are:

◊ Does your son's birthday make him one of the youngest or oldest children in the class?

◊ Would the retention be likely to produce long-term benefits? Surely the retention year would be easier for him, but what about subsequent years?

◊ Is he delayed in areas other than academics? What are his social skills like? What about his physical size?

◊ If he has siblings, how would that impact retention? If he would end up in the same grade as a sibling, sometimes that can cause conflict.

◊ What is the school's recommendation?

◊ If retention seems to be the best option, can you frame it in a positive way to your son?

Our experience has been that retention is easier on children than their parents. It is a complex decision that must not be taken lightly. Consideration should be given to repercussions for the retention year as well as its impact on the remainder of your son's school career.

Jason was a young man who seemed to be constantly in trouble with his teacher as well as his classmates. He seemed to have no patience with his work, throwing down his pencil or balling up his papers when he made mistakes. He had been able to keep up academically until third grade, when the reading required more concentration and the math involved more steps. He was in danger of retention, and he knew it. That seemed to fuel his anger. He got into trouble every day. His parents were upset that recess was being withheld from Jason because he had not completed his work. They felt, and rightly so, that he needed an outlet for his energy. He started lying about his homework, fighting with his siblings, and ruining most of the family's plans.

His family consulted with Jason's psychiatrist, who advised against any change in medication but did strongly recommend private behavioral therapy and an evaluation through the school district to determine if Jason also had a learning disability. The results of the evaluation indicated that he had difficulty with higher order thinking and was very concrete in his thinking. All of his academic skills were significantly below grade level, and his class work was at his frustration level. Jason subsequently qualified for services for a learning disability and received some of his academic instruction in a smaller classroom setting at his grade level. His parents reluctantly committed to private behavior therapy, which systematically targeted social skills and provided Jason with tools to use when confronted with difficult situations with his peers. Progress was slow and inconsistent, but Jason's parents could see that he was doing better. Without that significant intervention, Jason might have been retained, but his interest in school and his academic skills might also have continued their decline.

What to Do When There's No Progress

Even after diligent research, excellent communication, and support at home, your son may be struggling too hard in his current setting. If you feel he is not learning and/or is miserable, it is important to be proactive. Schedule a conference with the teacher and ask for his or her honest assessment of the situation. Together, brainstorm additional strategies or accommodations that could work. If your son is on medication, consult with the prescribing doctor to see if adjustments are in order. If a change is made in medication, sign a release for the teacher to communicate directly with the doctor to provide firsthand information about the effects of the medication during the school day.

Inquire if the school has any additional resources that can be tapped. Is there a guidance counselor or school psychologist who could observe your son and provide feedback? Sometimes fresh eyes may look at a problem from a different perspective and come up with solutions. Consult with the principal, since he or she is the instructional leader of the school. Changing teachers or classrooms is usually not an option but could be explored.

If no workable solutions are forthcoming, you could explore the advisability of changing schools. This should not be entered into lightly, because stability is important. However, sometimes the school/student match just doesn't produce the desired results and could end up damaging a student's attitude toward learning.

Time to Change Schools

How do you know when it's time to move your son to a different school? We know boys with ADHD have their ups and downs, but sometimes the bad times far outnumber the good ones. When this occurs, it may be a sign that it's time to change to a different school. In some cases, your son may be asked to leave a school. In our experience, this occurs most frequently during preschool. You may have been hoping that things would be different in elementary school because your son is slightly older and should have matured. This would be a welcome change, but your son's school troubles usually do not spontaneously disappear during elementary school. Remember, his ADHD is a condition that may be with him all of his life.

If your son is attending a private elementary school, there is always the chance that he may not be asked back for another school year. It can throw you into a tailspin when your son's private school informs you that he can't return. You may feel panicked, disappointed in your son or yourself, or discouraged that you must search for another school. If this happens to you, and even if it appears to be your son's fault, we recommend that you not blame him. It won't help the situation and will certainly hurt his feelings, reinforce that he failed again, and decrease his self-esteem. Yes, you want to have a straightforward conversation about his work habits, effort, and behavior, but rarely is it 100% your son's responsibility. Emphasize to your son that when a private school placement— or any school placement, for that matter—does not work out, it is always a combination of factors. Help your son recognize the important lesson from this experience so the two of you can avoid a repeat experience.

Sometimes leaving private school is a mutual decision between parents and the school, and other times it is your decision not to return. Some parents find a private education more limiting for their sons with ADHD, because private schools are not required to make as many accommodations as public schools and may have fewer resources. Although many private schools do make accommodations, it can vary widely by school. One client believed her son's private school was not doing enough and told us, "It was heart-wrenching to watch Joey struggle. He was aware he was considered different, and it broke my heart! I knew it was time for a move." Do you feel like your son is a square peg being made to fit into a round opening? It's time for a change if the match between your son and his private school is not correct.

In a public school, your son's ADHD may be tolerated more than in private school because of the student diversity found in most public schools. Exactly how much your son's ADHD behaviors are tolerated depends on his individual teacher. Some teachers have better classroom management skills and can handle when your son calls out answers, squirms while seated, picks away at his eraser, or jumps up for frequent trips to the pencil sharpener. Having a teacher who understands your son makes life better for everyone.

However, some teachers may not understand boys with ADHD. Try to help educate the teacher about your son and about boys with ADHD in general. Many teachers are willing to learn more about ADHD and techniques that they can use to help your son and to make their classrooms run more smoothly. When we diagnose a boy with ADHD, we give his parents information about ADHD that they can read and share with their son's teacher such as the Information for Your Teammates: Your Son's Teachers section included on pages 105–109 of this book. Other fact sheets are available on websites such as http://www.CHADD.org or other parent support websites.

Although your son's ADHD behaviors can't get him totally kicked out of the public school system unless he engages in some very serious behaviors, he can be placed in a special education self-contained classroom or expelled and sent to an alternative school. We discuss these types of placement in greater detail in Chapter 6. For now, just remember that the school staff must have your permission in order to place your son in a special education classroom or alternative school.

Sometimes things do not go well, despite your best efforts. If you've failed in numerous attempts to work with your son's teacher and engaged the principal, school psychologist, or guidance counselor to explore all options, and you still sense a growing despair in your son, then you may find it in his best interest to learn what other school choices might be open to him.

Ask yourself these questions:

◊ Am I receiving daily (or almost daily) phone calls about my son's school behavior?

◊ Is the majority of feedback I receive from my son's teacher or school negative?

◊ Has my son been suspended from school?

◊ On multiple occasions, have I been asked to come pick my son up early from school because of his behavior?

◊ Does my son say he hates school or does he feel sick each morning when it's time for school?

◊ Does my son's self-esteem seem low? Does he make statements such as, "I'm dumb. I'm going to drop out of school. My teacher doesn't like me. No one likes me."

◊ Does my gut feeling or intuition tell me it's time for a change?

If you answered yes to the majority of these questions, it could be time for a change. If so, the next question is, "Where?" There are positives and negatives to any educational setting. Can you afford to send him to a private school? Does he need a special type of school? Should you homeschool or consider a virtual school? Often the answer is not obvious or easy.

If your son remains in the public school system, we recommend you talk to his principal to gain his or her support for making next year's teacher a good match with your son. Emphasize your son's strengths, needs, and the type of teaching style you believe works best for him. Although most principals cannot honor every parent request, many will listen carefully to what you have to say, especially about a child with a disability. Make an appointment and take notes to share. It's always helpful to have another person with you when meeting with the principal or school staff. Bring along your spouse, a friend, or an advocate.

Jim's Experience With Switching Schools

Jim's son, Teddy, attended public school from kindergarten through second grade, and it was generally a good experience. At the end of Teddy's kindergarten year, the school wrote a 504 plan, which allowed reasonable accommodations for his ADHD. This plan was helpful because it provided that Teddy should be allowed to stand up and complete his work, be sent on an errand if he appeared to need movement, not have all of his recess taken away if he failed to complete his class work, and receive a reduced homework load. Teddy's second-grade teacher understood that boys with ADHD required movement, and she allowed Teddy to have a two-seat option. He was able to work either at his desk or at the table in the back of the room. He enjoyed this option because it provided choice, and at times one seat felt better than the other one.

At the end of second grade, Jim and his wife decided to move Teddy to a private school. Although the public school's third grade had a good reputation, they were very concerned about the mandatory third-grade retention if Teddy didn't pass the high-stakes state test. At this age, Teddy had the characteristics of many boys with ADHD—he rushed through his work and gave up quickly if the work became too challenging. Jim and his wife believed Teddy would rush through the state test, possibly facing mandatory retention if he did poorly.

When considering the move from public to private school, Jim and his wife weighed the pros and cons. Some aspects in favor of private school included:

◇ no mandatory third-grade retention,
◇ smaller class size,
◇ a more accepting environment,
◇ daily recess,
◇ lots of parent involvement, and
◇ manageable amounts of homework.

For their family, the only drawbacks were paying tuition and providing transportation.

The first private school they visited wasn't a good fit. After Teddy took the admissions test, the principal told Jim and his wife that the school couldn't meet Teddy's needs. Although they were disappointed, Jim and his wife kept the positive perspective that they would find the right place for Teddy. As it turned out, Jim and his wife located a faith-based private school that offered small classes, structure, and a supportive learning environment. The principal openly accepted Teddy and his ADHD and willingly honored the 504 plan that was already in place, allowing a smooth transition between schools. Teddy successfully attended this elementary school from third through fifth grades.

Home and Community Issues

You know by now that your son doesn't leave his ADHD at school. He faces challenges at home, around the neighborhood, and in any activity he pursues, because ADHD permeates all areas of a boy's life. It is also common for boys with ADHD to have difficulties when interacting with their siblings and peers.

Siblings

If your son with ADHD has brothers and sisters, you understand there are times they fight like cats and dogs and other times they laugh like best friends. The sibling relationship is important for boys with ADHD because it helps them learn to form appropriate interpersonal relationships. Home is usually where boys with ADHD feel safest because of the unconditional love within a family. Therefore home is a great place to start teaching your son with ADHD how to appropriately interact with his siblings and others.

Most boys with ADHD require your specific advice and instruction to learn how to get along with their siblings. Forming solid, civil relationships does not come easily to most boys with ADHD, and siblings often find their brothers with ADHD annoying, interfering, and difficult. Sure, a lot of brothers and sisters find each other annoying, but boys with ADHD can seem off the charts. You must make it a priority to teach your son courteous and friendly behavior and provide him with opportunities to apply what he's learned with his siblings.

We recommend that you establish this primary family rule: "Treat others with respect." This directive must come from parents; after all, you are the head of the family. Your message must be, "We are a family. We treat each other nicely and we support each other." Teaching mutual respect starts with you. Model it and live it—and that means treating your children with respect and requiring that they treat you and one another with respect as well. Establish it as a theme in every family talk, especially when that discussion involves conflict. If this message isn't firmly established during the elementary years, adolescence can be very difficult. If you expect your son with ADHD to respect you and the other family members, then you must first show that same respect to him. He has to know what it looks like.

We understand that this can be so hard to do. Boys with ADHD sure know how to push your buttons, don't they? Young boys with ADHD often react with noises (including body noises) rather than words because they feel emotions much faster than they can label and speak them as words. We've known boys who, when reprimanded for behavior, will do things like stick out their tongues, make a "raspberry" sound, say "la la la la la," or sing song lyrics. If your son does this to you, try to remember how primal his first reaction can be. When you ask him to stop the unwanted behavior, follow it up by saying, "Use words instead of noises."

Name-Calling

When you establish the family rule "treat others with respect," you take an important step toward creating family peace. Name-calling falls in the category of disrespectful behavior you're likely to have to address with all of your children, but your son with ADHD may need extra patience in learning that ugly names are absolutely not part of your family's vocabulary. This means you don't ever call your son an unkind name, and he never calls you or any of his siblings a mean or profane name. Agree on consequences and enforce them. This is one of Jim's most important family rules. In addition to the standard consequence, he and his wife also make each child pay a dollar any time there is name-calling. It simply won't be tolerated, and this extra consequence really made the "treat each other with respect" rule hit home.

Counseling

Occasionally, sibling disagreements become so intense that the situation requires the help of a mental health counselor, family therapist, or psychologist. Family discord often makes everyone feel miserable, and this feeling spills over into your son's life at school, at his friends' homes, and everywhere he goes. Often within a half-dozen or so sessions, a well-trained counselor can help turn around family problems. In our experience the time and money you spend working with a professional is time and money invested in family harmony.

Friendships

Some boys with ADHD are gifted communicators. If your son has this talent, continue to develop it, because it will carry him far in life. Others boys have communication and social difficulties because they speak before they think—which tends to get them in hot water. Other boys with ADHD seem to have difficulty processing language, which impacts their social skills. Many boys with ADHD don't think of others or about the way others perceive them. Sometimes, boys with ADHD will pass gas as we're testing or talking with them. It just happens. One time a boy said to Jim, "I like your head. How'd you get it so shiny?" A little boy asked Mary Anne, "How did you get so old?" Often, whatever's on their mind or in their body just comes out. This is part of what gets them into trouble. Professionals call this "lack of inhibition," because boys with ADHD often don't have the little voice in their minds that says, "Don't do that, because it could get you in trouble," or "Don't say that, because it could hurt someone's feelings." They don't hold back their automatic thoughts. The words or actions just happen. So the next time he gets into trouble and you ask, "Why did you do that?" and hear him reply, "I don't know," he's probably telling you the truth. It just happened.

This brings us to another point: Asking your son the question, "*Why* did you do that?" is rarely helpful. We like the advice from Pete Wright (2009), an attorney and parent of two successful boys with ADHD and learning disabilities. He wrote,

When my children misbehaved or messed up, I never asked them, "*Why* did you . . ." When the parent asks a child "why," the child learns to create good excuses, shifts blame onto others, views himself or herself as a "victim of circumstances"—and does not learn to take responsibility for his or her behavior.

Talking about why the child misbehaved will not teach the child that he has control over himself, his environment, and his future. This will not teach him to take responsibility for his actions. When you ask "why," it's easy to slip in some guilt—"Why did you do this? You upset me so much. You made me feel terrible." Ask these four questions instead:

◊ What did you do?

◊ What are you going to do about it?

◊ To ensure that this does not happen again, what should we do to you now?

◊ If this does happen again, despite your good intentions now, how much more severe shall the punishment be next time? (para. 7)

If your son's ADHD is on the severe side, you may find that he's excluded from birthday parties and other social events. Some boys with ADHD have such aggressive behaviors that other kids become fearful of their impulsive behaviors. This happened to Teddy when he was 6 and 7 years old. Unbeknownst to Jim, Teddy was reacting impulsively by punching kids instead of telling them to stop teasing him. It escalated to the point that Teddy was excluded from a few play dates and gatherings. When Jim asked one of the dads about it, the father explained that the other kids were concerned about Teddy's impulsive behavior, and they never knew if he was going to haul off and hit them. Jim and his wife learned that allowing Teddy to play with one child at a time worked out much better than playing with a group, because there was less conflict. For quite a while, they structured Teddy's social life so they were there to watch him play or only allowed him to play at his own home with one child at a time. Soon Teddy matured and outgrew the hitting phase. Mary Anne's son wasn't aggressive to others but benefited from structured play dates organized around common interests.

Whenever conflicts with other children arise, you need to listen to your son with ADHD. He is often telling you the truth. Over time you can learn to recognize when he is being honest. Jim's wife has some type of "truth radar" and can always accurately identify when Teddy is telling the truth, because he becomes very emotional and insistent. Perhaps you recognize these types of signals from your son. Does he have certain behaviors that signal when he's being sincere? As a parent, watch your son for nonverbal cues and pay attention to his actions as well as his words.

Sports

Many boys with ADHD are naturally athletic and excel in physical activities and sports. It becomes a natural outlet where they can showcase their talents. Competing in sports may help your son with ADHD build a sense of accomplishment that could be missing from the academic areas of his life. Sports provide your son with focus, structure, and discipline. One of Jim's young clients struggled academically throughout elementary and middle school but always excelled in sports. During high school, he was so accomplished that he was the top player on his football team and landed a college scholarship playing football. This young man's motivation to play football was instrumental in his maintaining his grade point average for athletic eligibility.

From a very young age, Jim's son, Teddy, had amazing agility and could climb anything, especially trees and playground equipment. At the park, Teddy would climb to the top of the monkey bars, stand up, and walk across them as if he were on a high wire. Other playground moms would comment, "Look at that boy. That's so dangerous." Jim and his wife knew Teddy would not fall—and he didn't. As Teddy grew older, this agility helped him excel in skateboarding. Mary Anne's son was an outstanding athlete. Sports provided an important outlet for his excess energy, provided a vehicle for making friends, and kept him interested in school. He knew he didn't like sitting at a desk in class, but his love for recess and physical education made the school day worthwhile in his eyes.

We believe one secret to parenting boys with ADHD is determining if your son has a passion for sports. Expose him to different sports opportunities from a young age. As soon as he is eligible, enroll him in organized youth sports. Try T-ball, basketball, golf, tennis, roller or ice hockey, football, skateboarding, swimming, running, or martial arts. Once you find a sport where he has an interest and natural talent, build upon it. It does not matter whether it is a group or individual sport. Many boys we have worked with have been helped tremendously by karate, which stresses listening, discipline, respect, and following directions.

Compliment your son's athletic ability in front of others. Remember to tell him you are proud of him, and encourage him to stick with it and practice. Jim's son Teddy enjoyed playing baseball; starting at age 4, he played for eight seasons. Together they spent hours in the backyard throwing, catching, and hitting. During Teddy's first season of kid-pitch baseball, he hit a homerun. Jim was so proud of Teddy that he ordered a trophy topped with a baseball player and engraved with "My First Homerun" and the date. Teddy was so proud of himself and the trophy that for a while, it became a kitchen centerpiece. Although the trophy was nice, the recognition was the most important part of this experience.

Many boys with ADHD jump from sport to sport because having a short attention span is part of their disorder. They find a sport and become passionate about it but lose the passion just as quickly.

You can be the one to help your son persevere. Most importantly, if your son starts a sport, do not allow him to quit until the season is over. Although quitting is often the easy way out, it does not build his character. Even if your son believes he is the worst player on the team, don't let him bail on his team. Let your son earn the feeling of accomplishment and satisfaction that comes from sticking it out until the end. Teach him to push through when things get tough. Pushing through tough times goes against everything he naturally wants to do, but he needs to develop this ability for success in school and sports. Mary Anne's son enrolled in competitive swimming because of how much he enjoyed recreational swimming. However, he hated the rigor of the swim practices, even though he was a natural at backstroke. As a young child, he would cry about going to practice but was encouraged to stick it out until the session was over. He learned that once you commit to something, you have to see it through.

Remember, it is also okay if your son does not like sports. It may be hard for a dad to accept that his son is not going to have the same sports passion that he had as a youngster, but that may be the reality. Not every boy with ADHD is going to become a sports fanatic. If your son has tried group and individual sports but still does not have the knack for any of them, then you know more about his gifts and personality and can nurture his other talents.

Camps

Attending a day or sleep-away camp can build your son's confidence. Mary Anne's son attended recreational, Boy Scout, and church camps—all of which provided good lessons in being organized and keeping up with his belongings. Jim's son attended day camps during the summer. Many boys with ADHD enjoy camps that offer outdoor or hands-on activities. Jim's area is full of camp opportunities, and some of Teddy's favorites included fishing, surfing, and baseball camps. You know your son best and understand the type of camp he'd enjoy most. However, it takes due diligence on your part to locate just the right type of camp for your son.

Sure, any parent can sign their son up for a camp and send him off, but it's different for boys with ADHD. You know his camp must be just the right fit, have the right type of activities, number of children, staff personality, and structure—or it could be a disaster. He'll come home early, say he hates camp, won't want to return, and give you a hard time. You know that if he feels miserable, some of it is going to rub off on you too.

In addition to more typical summer camps, some locations offer therapeutic camps for boys with ADHD. Dr. Bob Field operates the California-based, multisite Quest Therapeutic Camps for children with ADHD and other associated disorders. If you choose a therapeutic camp for your son, you want to make sure it offers a process similar to what Dr. Field describes below.

In a personal correspondence, Dr. Field explained that his Quest camps are fun for kids and based on parental input and an individual screening assessment. Each camper receives an individualized treatment plan that helps address his most consequential problematic behaviors. The campers identify and understand specific behavioral goals. Using camp activities, therapy staff is able to observe difficulties as they occur and provide interventions right then and there. Counselors are advanced college or graduate students trained to help campers gain awareness as behaviors occur. In addition, during each hour of the day, campers receive specific staff feedback about the positive and negative aspects of their behavior. Campers are awarded points each hour based on their effort. As a camper progresses, higher points require increased effort, developing greater success. Combining a cognitive behavioral therapy approach and specially developed neurocognitive strategies, Quest's small-group therapy sessions facilitate the individualized goals of each camper. This model has been proven to successfully address problematic behaviors and help campers develop appropriate social skills.

Before you send your son to either a day or sleep-away camp, you need to think about a few important considerations:

1. Can I handle the stress of sending him off on his own?
2. Is he mentally prepared for camp?
3. What is the camper-to-counselor ratio?
4. What experience do the counselors have working with boys with ADHD?
5. How is discipline handled?

If your son is attending a sleep-away camp, ask the camp staff these questions:

1. How do you handle bullying?
2. What happens if my son wets the bed?
3. Who keeps and administers his medication?
4. What happens if there is a medical emergency?
5. Are electronics allowed?
6. How can I communicate with my son?
7. What efforts are made to help children make friends?
8. What if he wants to come home early?

In addition to thoroughly researching and selecting the best choice for your son, mentally and emotionally prepare him for the experience. As mentioned previously, boys with ADHD do not tend to like unexpected change. Explain what a typical day at camp is like. If the facility is located close to your home, stop by and introduce him to the director. Try to anticipate his feelings the first day of camp and give him words of encouragement that he can replay in his mind through the day. If your son is nervous about new situations and does not know any other campers, you might say something like, "On the first day of camp, a lot of kids won't know anyone. They may not look nervous on the outside, but I'll bet they feel nervous inside. Remember that and talk to lots of kids, because they are hoping they meet a good friend like you."

These types of simple steps set your son up for a successful camp experience.

Video Games

If you have a son with ADHD who doesn't love video games, he's one of the few. Video games are a part of life for most boys with ADHD, because the game often gives them feelings of control and success. The fast pace and stimulation they produce feel great to a kid with ADHD. Quite frequently we are asked our opinion on whether boys with ADHD should be allowed to play video games at all. Parents worry, "Are video games bad? Should we limit his video game time? Should we ban war types of video games?"

For many people it comes down to personal belief. We know that some parents ban their sons from playing all games except those with an "E" rating, for "Everyone." Other parents only allow video games on the weekend if the boy had a good week in school. Others allow their son 30 minutes each day once his homework is complete. Some allow unlimited play because it occupies his time and gives them some respite. As one mom stated, "I was never into video games so I don't understand the big obsession with them, but it gives him an outlet where he can chill. Actually, it helps him decompress from a hard day at school."

How you use video games is personal preference. Because the research is mixed on boys with video games, Jim's rule of thumb is to allow boys with ADHD some time to play video games because they can be a great reinforcement for good behavior. There are countless times when Jim has said to Teddy, "If you want to play your game, then I need your help doing so and so," or, "If you finish your homework without arguing, then you can play your game for 30 minutes." Nevertheless, Jim strongly recommends that parents use discretion with the amount of time they allow their sons to play. As we outline in Figure 6, video games have pros and cons, but too much video gaming is not a good thing. Jim suggests limit-

Pros	Cons
Can be used as a reinforcement tool	May hyperfocus on the game
Some games promote physical or mental exercise	Some games are violent
Can develop hand-eye coordination	May become emotional or defiant when it's time to stop
May become a hobby that leads to employment	Video games can be expensive
May build focus and concentration	May spend too much time gaming
May build feelings of success	May engage in less physical activity and have fewer opportunities for socialization

Figure 6. Pros and cons of video games.

ing video game time to a maximum of 2 hours on the weekend and 30 minutes on weekdays, if at all. We do not endorse allowing boys to play without limits.

Boys with ADHD are stimulated by the games' visual effects, real-life graphics, and intense action. Over and over we've heard a parent tell how her son becomes so hyperfocused on his game that he doesn't respond when called for dinner, he ignores his friends, or he doesn't notice when the phone rings. Does this sound familiar? When you tell him to stop gaming, he becomes agitated or irritable and begs for 5 more minutes. When you return, he becomes more defiant, and you become so provoked that you just reach over and pull the plug. He yells because you made him lose his level. Clearly defining the amount of game time, rules for stopping, and consequences for arguing help prevent this type of scenario. Boys with ADHD don't like new rules or things sprung on them, so with video games, and in everything you do, try to establish guidelines and procedures beforehand.

Self-Esteem

Think about your son's self-esteem. Does he appear to feel good about himself, or is he down in the dumps? When we complete an evaluation with clients, we believe it is important to assess a boy's self-esteem as part of the total process. Some psychologists see self-esteem as inconsequential, but we believe that if a boy has low self-esteem, then it permeates all areas of his life. If you work with a psychologist, our recommendation is to choose one who will assess your son's self-esteem. In our practices, we use a self-esteem measure that each boy completes independently, leading to a mixture of results.

If your son's self-esteem appears solid, you are fortunate. His self-esteem will help provide him with the confidence he needs to navigate life. Continue to nurture his self-esteem, because it can give him a sense of resiliency, which he'll need to bounce back when he has a setback or challenge. It will allow him to stand up, brush himself off, and try again. This is an invaluable quality to develop. If you want to learn more about instilling this sense of resiliency in your son, we recommend *Raising Resilient Children: Fostering Strength, Hope, and Optimism in Your Child* by Drs. Robert Brooks and Sam Goldstein, because it is full of ideas for developing resiliency and self-esteem.

The self-esteem of many boys with ADHD is low. It can become low because of repeated failures, constant reprimands from adults, teasing from peers, or just because of the way he is wired. What we call "global self-esteem" comprises your son's behavioral, anxiety, popularity, physical, and general satisfaction in life self-esteem. You may find your son's self-esteem is high in one area and lower in other areas. In our experience, boys with ADHD often have low behavioral self-esteem, which means your son knows he frequently gets in trouble. We also find that many boys with ADHD have lower anxiety self-esteem, which implies that they feel nervous about school-related tasks such as taking a test or being called on by the teacher. They act up in school and become the class clown to try to build confidence by making people laugh.

Your son's low self-esteem stifles his decision-making ability. Some boys with ADHD can't make even the simplest decisions. If your son thinks poorly of himself, then over time he may become anxious, frustrated, or depressed. These depressed thoughts create depressed actions, which lead to poor performance. Unchecked, it can become a difficult cycle to end.

If your son has low self-esteem, his automatic reaction to a new task that appears challenging is probably, "I can't." For many boys with ADHD, this "I can't" attitude turns into what professionals call "learned helplessness." Your son learns that it benefits him to become helpless. This develops over a period of time, because when your son automatically says, "I can't," many parents and teachers spring to complete the task for him. What you must do is determine if your son's problem is an "I can't" or an "I won't" type of problem. This allows you to decide how quickly you should step in to help. If it is an "I won't" problem, then you need to wait and let him try to work through it on his own. If the problem is "I can't," then you should step in, provide instruction, and step away to let him try. You want to do this to teach your son an "I can and I will" attitude.

You can help strengthen your son's self-esteem by affirming him in front of others. So often we reprimand and correct our son around other people, but we affirm him much less. Regardless of his age, your son needs to hear your encouragement and positive reinforcement, and he needs others to hear you giving it to him. He needs to hear you say statements like, "I'm proud of you. Your performance was awesome. You have a great heart. I love you." If parents don't affirm their son in this way, then he will find another way to get that affirmation, usually from peers or by smoking, drinking, or engaging in other dangerous behaviors. Is that what you want your child to do? Surely not. Build your child up by telling family or friends a positive story about him, send them an e-mail with a photo or a great story about him, or simply send him a note in his lunch box that he can read.

These are additional suggestions you can use to help develop your son's self-esteem:

◊ When age appropriate, explain his ADHD and help him understand it.

◊ Read age-appropriate books about self-esteem with your son. Search online booksellers with keywords such as "self-esteem children."

◊ Engage him in extracurricular activities (e.g., music, art, drama, sports, computers) where he can find success.

◊ Be aware of your positive-to-negative comment ratio, and increase your genuine praise.

◊ Comment on his positive qualities rather than his negative ones.

◊ Try to reduce family conflict by establishing routine, consistency, and structure.

◊ Help him identify and build at least one good friendship.

◊ Try to help him establish a positive relationship with his teacher.

◊ Identify a mentor (e.g., at school, within a club or other organization) who takes a special interest in your son and helps build him up.

◊ Work with a counselor.

Points to Consider

1. You can expect the elementary years to be challenging for you and your son. The demands of school shine a new spotlight on his deficits in executive functioning skills and his difficulties with behavior, focus, and attention. Do you recognize these weaknesses?

2. Are you keeping a problem-solving perspective? Seek professional help when necessary and never give up.

3. How involved are you? Your son needs you to be involved at school to advocate for him and to work with his teachers to create interventions that will help him succeed at this critical time in his life.

4. Because your son is different than every other boy with ADHD, he requires interventions tailored to his needs. What do you have in place for him?

5. Is your son in a school and classroom where his needs are being met?

6. Your son's challenges spill over into family and community life. Are you helping him be his best self?

Action Steps

1. If you have not already done so, establish daily (or at least weekly) communication with your son's teacher.

2. Monitor your son's academic progress. Supplement where necessary.

3. Make sure you have a workable homework plan in place.

4. Try some of the techniques in this chapter to create a healthy home and community environment for your son.

5. How is your son's self-esteem? What steps are you taking to develop his confidence?

6. Provide supports to help him grow in his ability to self-regulate his behavior.

Chapter 5

The Teenage Years

Your son is changing. His body is changing. His voice is changing. His emotions are changing, sometimes from minute to minute. He's entering that unfamiliar, sometimes unsettling phase of life—adolescence.

The adolescent and teen years are filled with new experiences and new responsibilities. Imagine your son walking down the hall of his new middle school or high school. Pretty girls are everywhere. The hallways are covered with posters for clubs he can join. It's loud. Inside each classroom there's a different teacher, and he knows the work is going to be hard. He's got a locker, and he's got to remember the combination and where it is and which books and notebooks to bring to which class. He's nervous. Or excited. Or scared. Or confused. Or all of those things.

This is a critical time for you to stay closely tuned in to your son. Because he has ADHD, you already know change can be a challenge for him. This is a time in his life when all of his familiar routines will be upset. He'll need to develop new strategies for success, and he'll need your help and support.

You can expect that this will be a time of tremendous growth but not just for your son. As he learns to become an independent young man, your role transitions as well. You'll continue to be his biggest fan, his advisor, and his sounding board. But now, it's also your job to look for ways to start letting go.

School Issues: A Time of Transition

Your son has many strengths that he'll take into his middle school and high school experience. Remind him of this, and take the time to explore areas you may not have considered before. Is he an especially sharp observer? Does he have an exceptional memory for intricate details? Is he gifted in music or art or math?

More and more, he'll have opportunities to use and develop his special talents and abilities. Everyone's different, but certain strengths have been identified in many individuals with ADHD. Maybe your son falls among them, if he's:

◊   a creative thinker,

◊   a good negotiator,

◊   highly intelligent,

◊   willing to take a risk to achieve a positive outcome,

◊   intuitive and perceptive, and

◊   able to focus intently on a subject or topic of extreme interest.

As a student with ADHD enters the upper grades, teachers and parents often dwell on the struggles he's likely to encounter. It's important that you regularly remind your son of how he's unique. Encourage him to find ways to use and develop his natural gifts in the more adult world he's about to enter.

And it is a more adult world. In elementary school, the focus is often on the child. In middle school, the focus moves away from the student and onto the curriculum. With his ADHD, it's likely your son has trouble remembering things, paying attention, organizing his time, and controlling himself. Success in higher education requires memory, attention, organization, and self-control—the very things that can be so difficult when you have ADHD.

There's a fairly straightforward explanation. These are all skills that can come with maturity. Depending on the severity of their ADHD, boys may be delayed by as many as 4 years in those kinds of problem-solving, attention, and memory functions that they need in a middle school or high school setting. Their social development may be similarly delayed. At one time, researchers studying ADHD believed that most children "outgrew" ADHD. Now we know that's not the case. Not all children with ADHD continue to be impaired into their teen years but a majority of them do. Many carry those challenges into adulthood as well. So you can see how important it is for boys to equip themselves with strategies they may need to use their entire lives.

As schoolwork gets more challenging and demands grow greater, the performance gap between students with ADHD and their friends without ADHD tends to widen. That can begin to happen in middle school. Sometimes, it doesn't manifest itself until high school, where there's even more to juggle, a quicker pace, and often, a less-friendly schedule. So, just as you've worked hard to make your son's elementary years unique, you and your son need to form a team to tailor his middle school and high school educational experience.

Middle School

Your son is not a little kid anymore. In fact, he probably reminds you of that on a regular basis. As your son leaves the comfortable and more nurturing environment of elementary school, you naturally hope his past successes will carry over into his new learning environment.

Remember that middle school will be a chance for him to grow, to make different friends, and to try interesting things. He'll hopefully be surrounded by people who are going to be eager to give him a chance to shine. If he's experienced frustrations or problems before, it's a chance for him to start fresh. Your son probably takes a lot of cues from you. It's a big step, but if your first response is fear, it's very likely you'll convey that to your son, and he'll become worried and nervous, too. It's true that there will be challenges—there will *always* be challenges for a boy with ADHD and for his parents. But do your best to reassure him that you're prepared, and that he will be too.

Multiple Teachers

This may be the first time your son is changing classes and having more than one primary teacher. Suddenly, keeping in close communication with your son's school just got six or seven times harder. How will you manage it?

Many parents begin planning the transition to middle school many months in advance. You may request to meet with school administrators and guidance counselors to discuss the curriculum and teacher selection and to let your son introduce himself. More and more, your son needs to be involved in school meetings and speak on his own behalf. This will be easier for some students than others. Still, encourage your son to contribute. It's a skill he'll need to practice.

You may find you have less input on teacher selection as your son moves into the upper grades. Instead of making specific requests, you may wish to express your preference that your son be assigned to a specific "type" of teacher. This won't only benefit your son but in the long run, the teacher and the class as well.

Generally, boys with ADHD do better with teachers who are:

◊ *Flexible:* This teacher grants extensions when your son misunderstands a homework assignment, leaves his work at home, or simply forgets to do it.

◊ *Open to modifying assignments:* This teacher understands that the goal is to have the student grasp the ideas and concepts she teaches. If a student struggles with a long essay but can demonstrate command of the material another way, like making a video or an art project, she's willing to let him do so.

◊ *Knowledgeable about ADHD:* Some teachers have far greater understanding of the disability and what to expect of a student with ADHD.

◊ *Attentive:* This teacher takes note when his students seem to be falling behind, and alerts their parents. This is especially important when a student has ADHD and may not remember to keep his parents updated when he's having trouble.

◊ *Cooperative:* Some teachers are very willing to work with parents. Keeping lines of communication open remains important in middle school. Your ADHD son probably hasn't learned all of the skills he needs to be his own advocate. You'll need to stay in close touch with all of his teachers as much as possible.

Maintaining communication with multiple teachers doesn't have to be the overwhelming task it sounds. You will, however, have to do a little homework. We suggest taking the time to learn how each of your son's teachers prefers to communicate, and honoring that. One may have office hours on Fridays between 10 a.m. and noon. Another may wish to receive only e-mails or text messages. One may give you his cell phone number and invite you to call any time.

Be sure to establish a courteous, respectful relationship with your son's teachers and with the school's administration and guidance staff. Get to know them, and show your appreciation for the jobs they do. Together, you can form a powerful partnership on your son's behalf.

More Classes, More Work

In the confusion of changing from one classroom to the next, having to find books and notebooks and reports in his locker, and getting the right books in his backpack to take to the right classes, how's a kid with ADHD supposed to manage during the day? And what about Thursday night at 9:30, when he mentions the blockbuster science project that's due the next day? Here are a few coping skills:

◊ Establish a routine. Before school starts, get permission to walk the halls with your son. Map out a route for his daily schedule. Together, determine when it makes sense for him stop at his locker to drop off and pick up books. Color-coding books and notebooks can help him know at a glance what he needs for each class.

◊ Enlist a "coach." Someone at school may be willing to serve as your son's coach or mentor. This could be a favorite teacher, his homeroom teacher, a guidance counselor, or a teacher's aide. This person's role would be to help your son stay organized while at school and stay ahead of assignments and coursework. Your son and his coach may need to meet in the morning and again before the end of the day, once a day, or weekly. You'll know your son will have a little extra help staying on track. You'll also feel more confident that any small problems will be flagged before they become big problems.

◊ Find out about big projects early. Your son may be studying a half-dozen subjects with a half-dozen different teachers. There's a good chance you won't be kept personally informed on every single homework assignment. Keeping track of those needs to be his job. But you may wish to ask about any larger or more complex projects your son will be expected to complete during the semester or year. Boys with ADHD have a more difficult time with long-term planning and organizing multiple components. Larger school projects are going to require you and your son to establish a game plan. For the sake of your family harmony, you want to avoid unpleasant surprises—like learning about a 10-page paper with accompanying 3-D maps and video—the night before they're due.

The Handwriting Issue

Boys with ADHD show greater difficulty with handwriting and written work than in any other academic area. Your son's handwriting may be illegible, incomplete, and missing punctuation. He may take an hour to write one paragraph. As children advance in school, they need to develop the ability to rapidly transfer thoughts and ideas to paper without becoming distracted by changing their minds or fixing small mistakes. This is a skill that many boys with ADHD have not mastered by the time they've entered middle school.

If the issue of handwriting hasn't already been a source of frustration for your son, there's a chance it could happen now. Written assignments are getting longer. Note-taking is becoming more important. Your son will be asked to express himself through writing in almost every subject he studies. Simply the thought of sitting down before a blank sheet of paper can cause fear and anxiety in some children with ADHD. Help him minimize and move past his fears of handwriting in the following ways:

◊ Discourage the student from interrupting himself while he's writing. Instead, allow time when he's finished to correct his mistakes.

◊ Suggest that he read his work aloud. That can help him identify and correct any errors.

◊ Find a pen or pencil that feels comfortable in your son's hand.

◊ Allow him to use a computer for written work, even if you need to get special permission to do so. (Another plus: If he loses his work between home and school, it will be backed up on your hard drive!)

Setting Reasonable Expectations

You have a right to have expectations of your son. He has a right to expect certain things of you, too. Your son isn't perfect. You can't demand more than he's equipped to give. At the same time, don't ever expect complete failure. Most of all, don't assume that the things your son does are deliberately designed to drive you crazy. They're not.

What's reasonable to ask of your son? As he goes through middle school, you can make it clear that he is required to:

◊ Complete his homework on time, without a struggle.

◊ Get acceptable grades. You need to define, together, what acceptable looks like. If he's extremely gifted in one subject, he might be expected to maintain an A average in that class. In other areas, a solid C might represent success.

What's reasonable for your son to ask of you?

◊ Begin to release control. Allow him to make some mistakes, understanding that boys with ADHD tend to take quite a bit longer than other children to learn from their mistakes. Be patient. He will.

◊ Trust him. When he demonstrates that he can handle a little responsibility, allow him a little more.

High School

Much of what we've written about middle school holds true for high school as well. The academic and social challenges continue to increase year by year. If they hadn't kicked in before, his hormonal and physical changes are now readily apparent. He's a young man. But if ADHD is still impairing his functioning, certain skills and abilities haven't caught up to his lanky limbs and ceaseless appetite.

These are the years when a young person moves into independence and self-reliance. It's no different for a kid with ADHD, just more challenging in many ways. In fact, it may be even *more* crucial that your son learn to advocate for himself. This will be a major step for both of you, one of many during the teen years. But remember, your primary job as a parent isn't to get your son with ADHD through school. It's to prepare your boy to be a man.

Self-Advocacy

From the time they enter high school, we believe students should be present at all meetings that concern their disability. There may be obvious exceptions—conferences when other students' privacy is at issue. But your son is now old enough to be part of the discussion, and you need to let him answer the questions that pertain to him. Resist the urge to answer for him. As he becomes more comfortable in this role, it's possible he may attend such meetings without you.

It is appropriate for your son to initiate discussions with his teachers about his ADHD. Many teachers respond well when a young man approaches them directly about his disability. He should be prepared to describe what his ADHD means for him—

what it might look like in the classroom, the kinds of assignments that have been hard for him in the past, and what's helped him succeed. It might go something like this:

> Mr. Rodriguez? Can I talk to you for a couple minutes about something important? I don't know if you know this, but I have ADHD. It's an actual disability, something that's different in my brain that means I have trouble paying attention and remembering things the way other kids do. Sometimes in class you might see me daydreaming. It's not because I'm bored or because I don't want to learn. It's because I get distracted really easily. It's just part of the disability. Last year in history, Mrs. Williams gave me a copy of her notes before every class. That really helped me pay attention better. When we had a test, she also let me stay after school and answer my essay questions out loud. That really helped a lot because writing out long answers is really hard for me. I've lived with this for a long time, and I've learned what works for me. I don't mind talking about it, if I can answer any questions. Do you think we could work together on ways to help me learn so my ADHD doesn't get in the way?

Much of this, of course, depends on the severity of your son's ADHD and whether he has any additional learning disabilities that may require your more active involvement. And please don't misunderstand. We're not suggesting you abandon your son and let him figure out everything on his own. Nationwide, educators report that lack of parental involvement is a major frustration and causes setbacks for children with ADHD. By reading this book, you've already proven yourself to be a concerned and caring parent. We're simply advising you to step back when it's appropriate to do so and see how your son does when he gets the chance to take the reins.

Sleep and the High School Student

Most current research shows that a typical teenager's body is designed to stay up late into the night and sleep well into the morning. Our school systems, on the other hand, still run on up-with-the-chickens time. In many parts of the country, high school students are in class by 7 a.m. Studies suggest that half of all teens with ADHD have additional sleep challenges. They report finding it hard to quiet their brains and go to sleep. Their sleep can be restless, or they may wake frequently in the night. They often feel tired in the morning.

Your son can't learn well if he can't get proper rest. In addition to trying common-sense procedures at bedtime (e.g., no caffeine, no video games), you might explore the following:

◊ Establish a reasonable bedtime. Talk this through. For instance, he may observe that he often feels tired at about 10 but gets a "second wind" after 11. Together, you'll probably see that it would be wise for him to get to bed by 10:30 or 10:45.

◊ Don't start projects after a certain time. Whether they're school-related or just for fun, big projects can make a person with ADHD lose track of time. If he becomes absorbed, he might look up to see that it's 3 a.m.

◊ Get plenty of exercise. There's a lot to be said for taking a bike ride, a swim, or a run after school. Your son will work off the energy he stored up all day, and a tired body sleeps better.

◊ Arrange the school schedule to avoid groggy times. It may be possible to set up your son's school day so he has non-academic classes (e.g., PE, art, music) early in the morning, while he's waking up. Or schedule them for the end of the day if he tends to run out of steam.

Clubs and Sports

Extracurricular activities are a valuable part of the middle school and high school experience. Surrounded by girls and boys with similar interests, your son will have the chance to make new friends. This is especially important for those children with ADHD who struggle in social situations. He'll gain a sense of belonging. He'll have an outlet for the energy that builds up during the school day. His life will become more balanced as he gets to turn his focus temporarily from the challenges of school and homework. Kids with ADHD seem to want to be doing something all of the time, and extracurricular activities are a great, positive way to respond to that need.

We encourage parents to let their sons explore a wide range of activities, though not all at once. Try new things one or two at a time, and see what works for your son and your family. If a particular sport or group isn't a good fit, require that your son fulfill his commitment and then move on to something else. We've put together some guidelines for you and your son to consider:

◊ Be honest with coaches and group leaders about your son's ADHD. Many will be unfamiliar with the disability. They need to know what to expect from your son, and how (and when) to discipline him.

◊ Remember that every added activity is one more thing for your son's daily planner, and one more thing for him to remember. You probably already know that overloading a child with ADHD is a bad idea. Remember this when you're thumbing through his school's activity booklet or reading your city's online recreation flyer.

◊ Every boy with ADHD is different, but hand-eye coordination often tends to be less developed in these boys. This can make some team sports—like baseball and basket-ball—a challenge because they require agility in catching and throwing. Your son may have more success in sports that emphasize gross motor skills—swimming or track, for instance.

◊ If your son's ADHD impairment remains severe, he may still have difficulty paying attention to the rules of a game or the instructions of his coach. Talk through his choice of sports with him, and encourage him to choose sports and positions that are engaging. He might be a great soc-cer player but might not fare well at playing goalie, where there's a lot of down time.

◊ Getting regular daily activity is a great way to improve the quality of your son's sleep, which may help him do bet-ter at school. Even if team sports aren't his thing, he may enjoy sports like skateboarding, rollerblading, or surfing. The martial arts can help develop discipline. Explore lots of options, and stay open to trying them yourself. Sharing a common love of a sport can be a powerful relationship builder.

Homework and Studying

In the families we see, homework causes more conflict than any other issue. The parent-child relationship is volatile. Homework struggles lead to fights, nagging, exasperation, impatience, anger, and tears.

If you've spent years sitting beside your son at homework time, you're ready to turn the responsibility over to him. You wonder whether *he's* ready. You're eager to help him develop a study routine that works well for him. You want peace in your home.

That desire is neither unreasonable nor impossible. If everyone in your house dreads homework time, you need to believe it can change.

Why it's tougher with boys. If he's like most young men with ADHD, your son may have difficulty seeing homework as a worthwhile use of his time. To him, it's boring. He probably doesn't feel as though he learns much from it. Boys lack the maturity to recognize the long-term value of their efforts. He knows he's been expected to sit in a seat at school all day, quite contrary to his active male nature. Now he must sit some more.

Boys, especially boys with ADHD, can have a much more defeatist attitude toward school than girls. Girls with ADHD will overcompensate toward perfectionism. Boys with ADHD often simply "check out," especially if they've gone through years of struggle. Forty percent of boys with ADHD have additional learning disabilities, compounding an already serious problem.

Getting him off to a new start. Helping your son get organized is the first step toward breaking old bad habits. Far more than their friends without ADHD, kids with ADHD need a way to keep track of every assignment, every report, every project, every swim meet, and every band rehearsal. Help your son set up a homework area so all of the supplies he'll need will be within reach of a quiet, comfortable place he chooses.

We also suggest that you and your son spend some time brainstorming about an age-appropriate planner system he finds workable and interesting. Go shopping together and see what makes sense to both of you, based on his needs. He might think a new iPad would be just the thing, but if he tends to lose electronic gadgets, you're well within your right to suggest a less pricey alternative. Traditional paper planners are available in office supply stores. You can even download an app for his cell phone to keep him on track. *What* you get is far less important than *how* he uses it and *how faithfully* he uses it.

Once his system is in place, he won't have to spend a lot of time thinking about how to get started on his homework—he'll just do it. He won't spend 15 minutes looking for a pen, because his homework area will already be set up with everything he needs. He's ready to go.

Establishing new homework routines. Wise parents need to take steps to restore and protect family harmony during the middle school and high school years, especially with so many other changes happening all at once. That means eliminating homework battles and shifting the responsibility for homework to the child. If you have a middle schooler, this may be a gradual transition, but the goal is to have your son be as self-directed as possible.

Your new rules need to emphasize this point: Homework isn't an option. Once again, putting a new routine in place requires you and your son to collaborate. Here are some guidelines:

◊ Let him set the time he's going to do his homework every day. Help him find a way to stick to it, whether he has a wristwatch alarm, a computer alert, or some other reminder.

◊ Establish a workplace where distractions are minimal. Some students with ADHD say it helps them to have music playing or some sort of white noise on in the background. You can give your older son some leeway, as long as he's able to stay focused.

◊ Encourage your son to tackle his more difficult (or least favorite) homework assignments first.

◊ It's important that he be able to take short breaks. It may be effective for him to set small goals for himself (e.g., read one section, do 10 problems) and then assess whether he's fresh enough to continue. If he is, he sets another small goal. If not, he takes a short timed break.

◊ You are not to do your son's work for him. Make yourself available if he has questions, but do not correct his work when he's done. Simply check to see that it's finished.

◊ Investigate whether you can borrow or buy an extra set of textbooks for your home, especially if your son is prone to forgetting the books he needs. Perhaps the textbook can be found in a digital version online.

◊ If he continues to have a problem recording or remembering assignments, see if your son can organize a study group of friends who don't have ADHD. They can help remind him of work requirements. Hearing discussions of the material will also help him learn.

When he needs extra help. Your son may find that organization and routine are still not enough. If your son needs hours and hours to finish his homework every night, it may be time to bring in reinforcements. You want to be his loving parent, not a sentry who keeps him locked in his room at night slaving over his homework. Some solutions include:

◊ *A tutor:* If you can afford it, this is often a wonderful option for a student with ADHD. The one-on-one attention helps him maintain focus, and talking through the material is an effective learning method when a student has ADHD. Teachers and education professionals are obvious choices, but sometimes a special neighbor or college student can make a great tutor. A gifted tutor can build a strong relationship with your son, and will see his value and help him realize his abilities. No less important, if there are struggles over homework, they're on someone else's watch. You're not the bad guy any more.

◊ *An accommodation plan:* If your son is laboring over the sheer amount of homework he is given, ask his teachers about reducing his workload. With the appropriate paperwork (discussed in Chapter 6), he may be eligible for an accommodation plan. It may be acceptable for him to complete only the even-numbered math problems, for example, as long as he can demonstrate mastery of the concepts.

◊ *A deadline extension:* Occasionally, your son may need to ask for extra time to complete an assignment. If this is part of his accommodation plan, then it's already available for him to use. We stress that this should be the exception, rather than the rule. Many boys with ADHD tend to procrastinate, and being given extra time simply means their work piles up even more.

Planning for College and Career

Your son's high school years are the time for both of you to shift your focus from what's immediately before you to the future—college, career, life plans. It's a time for the boundaries to expand again.

In high school, your son will be given the opportunity to choose the classes he wants to take. He'll start to consider where—and whether—to go to college. He'll think about what he wants to do for a living. He'll need your guidance, along with the input of other wise mentors.

Encourage your son to think about college early, even during his freshman year. He'll feel your support, and it will help keep him focused on his goals and the reasons he continues to work so hard in high school. One of our clients, Nick, offered this advice to other teens:

> Use college as a goal for motivation and not to fail. You have one part of your brain that says give up, but the other half says you'll feel worse if you give up so you have to try your best. You have to identify where you are, identify what you want, and figure out how you are going to get there. Think of it as having a master plan.

Have Him Make a List of His Target and/or Dream Colleges

Not 30 schools. A half-dozen, maybe, and talk about why he's interested in them. Be objective and realistic. For instance, going to school 3,000 miles away from home is a legitimate draw for a young man seeking independence, even if it doesn't quite match what you're looking for in a curriculum. Make an appointment for the two of you to sit down with his high school guidance counselor and talk about what it's going to take to get into his target colleges.

Visit as Many Schools as Possible

Just being on campus, sitting in on classes, and talking to students will help him see that college isn't just an extension of high school. It's a different world. He'll need different, new skills.

Begin to Coach Him on the Life Skills He'll Need

Teach him to do his own laundry. Let him begin to navigate bureaucracy himself. He'll need to do those kinds of things, and many more, at college or when he's out on his own.

Help Him Stay on Track With His Classes

Teens with ADHD sometimes make impulsive choices. A student with ADHD might decide to take a class not because he's interested in it, but because his buddy is going to be in the class. In high school, the choices your son makes about his curriculum will start to affect his potential for admission to college in general, and to the colleges of his choice. He needs to understand what goes into wise, long-term decision making.

Home and Community Issues

As young people mature, society looks for them to take responsibility for themselves, for their actions, and for the choices they make. This extends across an ever-widening arc, from their social lives to the workplaces and onto the roadways. The troublesome part, as your son may know, is that teens with ADHD are still experiencing delays in impulse control, attention to detail, decision-making ability, problem solving, and social skills. In fact, they may be months or years behind their peers without ADHD. Your son still needs time, tools, and tactics to succeed.

Helping Your Son Win With People

What comes to mind when you think about the qualities that help you enjoy life? What about interacting and socializing with people? We believe our teens with ADHD must have good people skills in order to live life to the fullest. After all, building relationships is one of our primary functions as human beings.

We recommend *25 Ways to Win With People: How to Make Others Feel Like A Million Bucks* by Drs. John C. Maxwell and Les Parrott. It's packed with practical ways to build relationships. The book is easy to read and not at all dense or technical. It includes many stories to illustrate the 25 key points. And the book is small. It won't overwhelm teens who are immediately turned off by thick, textbook-style volumes.

We encourage parents, grandparents, aunts, uncles, and important adult friends to read the book ahead of time or together with the teen. This allows for important common ground. In other words, everyone has the same information. That opens the way for discussion and shared experiences or ideas. How might your family work this valuable book into your routine? Here are two ways you might do so:

1. Save this book for summer reading, when the academic demands of school lessen. Read the book in advance, and let your son know that over the summer he'll be reading an excellent and potentially life-changing book called *25 Ways to Win With People.* For the first 25 weekdays of summer, he'll read a chapter a day. Reassure him that the chapters average fewer than 7 pages. It will take 5 weeks to complete

the book. Each day, you'll ask him to write a short summary of the key points and discuss it with you.

For example, one way to win with people is to practice the "30-Second Rule." This rule simply states that within the first 30 seconds of a conversation, you say something encouraging to a person. Once your teen has presented his summary, ask questions about how he envisions himself using this rule. Teens with ADHD will understand this rule, but many won't know where to apply it. They will need a parent or adult's concrete guidance. If your son comes up blank, you might say something like,

> I bet you can use this rule when we are at the grocery store. When we check out, the cashier usually looks at us and smiles. I think you could offer that person encouragement by saying, "I'll bet you make a lot of people happy by being so friendly." Do you think you can try this?

Role-playing is another effective practice tool. You can practice his new skills within the supportive context of your home, where he shouldn't be as self- conscious as he might be in public.

2. Make learning and applying the 25 points a family project. Together, the family agrees to read one chapter per week. Some parents set aside part of the day on Saturday or Sunday to have a short talk about the key points. For the entire week each family member works on applying the step. Family members practice with each other as well as out in their school, work, or daily activities. If the family has dinner together, they should talk about their experiences.

Even though a new point is introduced each week, it's important to keep in mind that earlier points don't get discarded. Apply them as much as possible, especially if there are one or two you have found highly useful. This is what we call the "rent-to-own" philosophy. We are teaching our teenagers to try the point out (or rent it) for a week. If he finds it useful, he continues to rent it and use it. At some point your son may decide that this point is so helpful that he'll decide to own it and apply it on his own because he has recognized its value in his life.

This is exactly what happened when Jim's son Teddy read the chapter on "Be the First to Help." We discussed this point and practiced it, and he tried it out for the first week. At first he found it was hard to apply this in school, because he didn't want his friends thinking he was trying to be the teacher's pet. But then he did simple things like help a friend solve a tough math problem, pick up a girl's pencil when it fell on the floor, and stick up for a kid being called names. Teddy felt so internally rewarded that he said, "This is one way to win that really works like it's supposed to."

Clients typically report that the one-point-a-week method really helps the teenager understand, practice, and internalize the steps. Think about your family and decide which way would work best for you.

Getting a Job

Much like an extracurricular activity, finding a part-time or summer job can give your son a place where he can excel. There are many valuable skills and lessons he can learn in the workplace:
 ◊   employer, coworker, and customer relations,
 ◊   the importance of being on time,
 ◊   remembering and following directions,

◇   a sense of independence,

◇   money management, and

◇   building a resume for future positions.

If you and your son decide the time is right for him to find a job, talk through the kind of commitment it takes to be a dedicated employee. There are any number of entry-level jobs that are well-suited to a high-energy teen with ADHD, so take the time to help him find a job he can really get excited about. If he needs stimulation, a change of pace, and lots of physical activity, he should look for that in a job.

He may learn more than he expects. It's not unprecedented for a boy to decide he eventually wants to go into a line of work that doesn't require a college degree. That idea can be pretty appealing to a boy with ADHD, who may have spent years struggling in the classroom. Spending a summer mowing lawns or flipping burgers might change his mind about the value of continuing his education. It may also help him realize he *does* want to work with his hands in some way. In that case, he may want to investigate vocational training or trade schools, so he doesn't get trapped in a minimum-wage job as an adult. Keep encouraging him. *There are no careers a person with ADHD can't do.* Remind your son he has what it takes to pursue anything he's passionate about.

Remembering some of the difficulties he may have had with teachers, your son may be concerned about having a boss. If you can't meet the person in charge, make every effort to have your son meet the supervisor he'll work with before he accepts a job. He needs to feel comfortable that this person will be flexible and understanding. Depending on the severity of his ADHD, it's up to you and your son whether or not his employer is informed of your son's disability. Whether or not you inform the job, your son needs to feel that his supervisor will support him as he learns the job.

Because working, even part-time, will be a new challenge, be prepared to help your son succeed. He'll need to establish a new routine and may need to practice some new skills before he feels comfortable tackling this big step on his own. For instance, you can help him:

◊ Learn how to fill out a job application. Because boys with ADHD have trouble writing, filling out a handwritten application in person can be a traumatic experience. If you think that's going to be the case for your son, suggest that he ask permission to bring the application home and return it the following day. He can also investigate whether there's an online application option.

◊ Understand the interview process. If conversation is difficult for your son, practice this at home. He needs to be comfortable answering questions about himself. Together, you could role-play through a typical interview scenario: Why are you interested in this job? Can you tell me about your strengths? What experiences have you had working on a team? Your son should also have some basic questions about the job. This indicates his interest level to a potential supervisor.

◊ Learn to be on time. You may need to wake him up, or remind him it's time to leave for work, before it becomes his habit. You don't want him to lose the job as a consequence of being late. Having a job is a confidence-builder and an important step toward independence. Also, arriving at his job 5–10 minutes early should become part of his routine. Especially at the beginning, do whatever you need to do to help him with this. That might mean setting two alarm clocks, leaving reminder notes on his mirror, or having someone call or text him when it's time to get ready for work.

◊ Manage his clothing and work-related items. He may have a uniform or other gear he always needs to have with him at his job. Develop a routine to make sure his work clothes get laundered and the other items are ready to go when he is. A teen with ADHD is just as likely to misplace his plastic nametag as his homework.

◊ Work on his manners. No matter where he goes, your son will need to be polite to the people he encounters. It's likely they won't know him. They won't know the background of his ADHD. If he blurts out inappropriate remarks, interrupts people, or chatters to his coworkers, he'll jeopardize his job. Employers need to see the same kinds of self-control he's been working to develop in other areas of life. Help him by role-playing and talking through situations that didn't go well on the job.

◊ Show him how to be a team player. It's unlikely your son will be working alone. Having a job will be a wonderful experience for him to bring his unique perspective to a group effort, but he also has to be willing to consider other ideas and figure out how to work with people he might not like.

◊ Explain the value of extra effort. Your son is being paid to do a job. He can do it in an average way, or he can do it in an exceptional way that wins notice and praise and an increased sense of self-worth. Talk with him about ways he can give a 110% effort at his job.

Money management. Once your son has an income, he'll need your guidance in learning to manage his money. Together, you can begin to explore basic financial principles such as:

◊ how a checking account works and how to balance it,

◊ how compound interest works, and

◊ how to pay his bills and expenses on time. This is a little like homework. But in this case, if he fails to do it (or forgets), the penalty isn't failing the course. The consequences will be additional fees and eventually, a poor credit score. A thousand reminders from you may not be as effective as the first $35 late fee that comes out of his own pocket.

People with ADHD are especially vulnerable to spending their money impulsively. Saving is a very difficult concept for them to grasp because it's so abstract. Saving his money to buy something later is not nearly as stimulating as your son buying something— almost anything—right now. As he matures, he needs to understand that the concepts of self-control and delayed gratification apply to his finances as well. Depending on the severity of your son's ADHD, he might be months or years behind his peers in his ability to handle his money soundly.

It's a fairly simple coping strategy, but if your son is saving for a big purchase, he should not take a wallet full of cash every time he goes with his friends to the movies or the mall. Restricted-access accounts, like long-term CDs, are a great place to park money meant for a car or another big purchase. Credit cards can be very difficult for a teen with ADHD to manage. They simply provide temptation to spend more than he has. If you feel your son needs to carry a card for emergencies, we recommend a card with a pre-paid balance or a debit card you monitor carefully. Show your son that you trust him with a small amount. You can increase his access as he shows that he can handle it.

Dating

Much of what has come your way on the ADHD journey may have been a surprise. In the area of dating and your son's sexual development, you can anticipate some of the changes that are to come. You can discuss them openly. You can make sure he is as well-prepared as possible.

If a boy has a level of discomfort around girls, how will he ever get up the nerve to ask one out? One key might be simply being around them more, and that can start long before he's of dating age. Many adolescent boys with ADHD benefit from participating in group activities with boys and girls. That helps dissolve some of the mystery and can help him feel more comfortable when the time comes.

Many boys begin to show interest in dating when they are 13 or 14. Because of their emotional immaturity, boys with ADHD still tend to act a little goofy. Girls don't generally like boys who still act so silly, so your son may not be ready to date until he's 15 or 16. Whatever his chronological age, though, you need to discuss your family's dating rules beforehand. This will help him know what to expect when the time comes. These include:

◊ When he can go on dates and how often. You'll likely have different rules for the school year and for school holidays and the summertime.

◊ Who can he date? What if you don't know her? Typically, he'll date a friend from his school, church, or community. But he might wish to date someone you don't know. Ask to meet her.

◊ Where they're going, what they'll be doing, and whom they'll be with. Your responsibility to your teenage son doesn't end simply because he's on a date. If you would not permit him to attend unsupervised parties alone, he shouldn't be allowed to take a date to one.

◊ Guidelines for when his girlfriend comes to your house. His girlfriend should be welcome in your home. Whether you approve of her or not, make her feel comfortable. If she's not the girl for him, he'll figure it out eventually. But he's never to have her over when he's home alone, and you'll probably want to limit the time they're alone together in a room with closed doors.

◊ What if he breaks a rule? Your son needs to know in advance that he will face consequences for breaking one of your rules about dating. Dating is a privilege that shows you trust him. If he loses that trust, take away that privilege for a week or two, and then return it for a trial period. For boys with ADHD, a short removal of a privilege is as effective as a long one.

For teens with ADHD, the line between dating and sexuality is a fine one. Dr. Russell Barkley (2000b) has conducted exhaustive studies of children, adolescents, and teens with ADHD. His research is often shocking and showed that:

◊ Thirty-eight percent of teens with ADHD are involved in a pregnancy.

◊ Teens with ADHD begin having sexual intercourse earlier than their average peers.

◊ Teens with ADHD have more sexual partners and are less likely to use contraception.

Parents, sit up and take notice. You already know that boys with ADHD have little self-control. They can be impulsive. They find it difficult to delay gratification. So from a physical perspective, the temptation to have sex is powerful. And there's a strong psychological urge as well. Because the teen with ADHD is delayed emotionally, he may seek out behaviors that may make him seem more mature—including sex—in order to fit in. Because he has trouble projecting long-term consequences of his actions, your son won't be as affected by fear of fathering a child or the threat of contracting a sexually transmitted disease.

We urge you not to turn a blind eye to the possibility that your son is acting on his strong sexual urges. Here are some tools and guidelines to help him:

◊ Talk to him about the rest of his life. He may not understand that millions of teens contract STDs every year and that for many of them, like HIV and herpes, there is no cure. He will take them into every relationship he has and into his marriage. If he fathers a baby, it will forever change him, no matter the outcome of the pregnancy.

◊ Don't rely on school sex-ed classes alone. Anticipate the physical changes he's experiencing and discuss them openly. If this is impossible or difficult for you or him, make sure he has access to good resources he can read or watch. Just because your son has ADHD and has had difficulty with reading material, don't presume he won't read a book about sex. One of Jim's clients had success with Dr. James Dobson's book and CD series, *Preparing for Adolescence: How to Survive the Coming Years of Change.* The family was able to listen to the CDs together, discuss them, and talk through dating, peer pressure, and other physical and emotional issues.

◊ Make sure he knows your family's moral code. Many parents presume their sons know the code "Dating = Love + Respect." That can be a dangerous and false assumption. Boys, including boys with ADHD, don't always view their early sexual experiences as being associated with love and marriage. For them, it's more about excitement and maturity.

◊ He must understand that if someone says "no," he has to stop, no matter what has led up to that point.

A teen with ADHD has learned to expect his actions will be judged. Try not to judge him as he grows into the body of a man and explores dating, relationships, and his own sexuality. Instead, be available to discuss—calmly and thoughtfully—any issues that come up. Remember, you *want* him to come to you.

Driving

Another major milestone for your son will be when he slides behind the wheel of a car. It represents freedom, independence, and being on the brink of adulthood. For you, it represents a major loss of control. Unlike many of the other obstacles you've navigated, this one truly is a matter of life and death.

Once again, we rely on Dr. Barkley's research to suggest why parents of boys with ADHD are right to be concerned. Working with Dr. Daniel Cox, Barkley (2007) found that young drivers with ADHD are:

◊   2–4 times more likely to be involved in auto accidents,
◊   4 times more likely to get speeding tickets,
◊   3 times more likely to have injuries,
◊   4 times more likely to be at fault, and
◊   6–8 times more likely to have their licenses suspended.

It's hard to resist the temptation to assign cause for numbers like those. We know that distractibility and difficulty paying attention are traits of young boys with ADHD. It's dangerous if you can't focus when you drive. Teens with ADHD also have a need for highly stimulating activities like risky, high-speed driving.

Whatever the reason, you may have a sense that your son may not be able to handle the responsibility of driving when his friends without ADHD begin getting their licenses. This is common. Many teens with ADHD wait 6 months, a year, or more before pursuing their drivers' licenses. This allows them a bit of additional time to mature and develop the necessary skills to operate a vehicle safely.

Some parents tell us, "I dread teaching my son to drive. He's so sensitive to correction." That's a valid point. Think back to the time when you were learning to drive. How many times did your own mom or dad stomp on the floor of the passenger side of the car, hoping to find that a brake had miraculously appeared? It's tough for both of you. He'll be nervous and unsure. You'll be worried and tense. Remember, preserving your relationship is essential. This is a great time to enlist backup. If your school has a driver's education program, make sure he signs up. If it's in your budget, sign him up with a professional driving school. He's far less apt to act out with a stranger than he is with you. If that's not possible, maybe there's another trusted adult who'd be willing to teach him. Some communities and schools are even beginning to introduce high-tech driver simulation programs. Much like flight simulators, these machines expose inexperienced drivers to dangerous and unfamiliar situations to give them practice in safe driving techniques. They're expensive and not readily available, but they offer a wonderful way for learners to practice until they get it right, without risking anyone or anything in the process.

When you think your son may be ready to begin driving, here are some of the elements that need to be part of your family discussion:

◊ Do you believe your son is mature enough to drive? Does he?

◊ Does he feel ready to pass all of the parts of the driver's test? Does he need extra help with the written portion?

◊ Will he be expected to pay for the expenses associated with driving? Can he afford it?

◊ When he gets his license, how often will he be allowed to use the car? Will he be able to drive at night? In bad weather? With friends in the car?

◊ What happens if he breaks one of your rules?

This last point is an important one. You must have immediate, pre-established consequences for violating rules associated with his use of the car, and they need to be reasonable and proportionate. It's not reasonable to remove his car privileges altogether if he's a half-hour late getting home one day or if he forgets to fill the gas tank. That kind of offense might warrant loss of driving privileges for a week. But if you find he's been drinking and driving, the penalty needs to be strict and severe. He needs to know this.

The day your son earns his license is a day he'll never forget. It's an enormous step toward manhood, and he should feel very proud. Celebrate this moment with him. But also emphasize that driving is a privilege, not a right. He needs to earn and continue to earn the privilege of driving a car.

As explained by Katz (2007), Dr. Russell Barkley has recommended a three-tiered graduated system for newly licensed teens with ADHD. We believe this is a fine idea. It allows your son to become more comfortable—and safer—behind the wheel. It also gives him time to earn your trust before you permit him more responsibility. Here's a basic summary of Dr. Barkley's ADHD Safe Driving Program:

◇ Level I (0–6 months)
   ♦ He drives only during the daytime

◇ Level II (6 months–1 year)
   ♦ He drives during the daytime and until 9 or 10 p.m.

◇ Level III (after he's had his license for 1 year or more)
   ♦ Unrestricted driving according to parents' rules

It's also recommended that a reminder of your family's driving rules be posted prominently in the car your son drives (Katz, 2007). Especially in the case of a young driver with ADHD, it's important to see that reminder every time he gets behind the wheel. We recommend that your list include the following:

◇ Absolutely NO alcohol or drugs.
◇ Keep music low.
◇ No wearing headphones.
◇ No texting. There are, in fact, mobile phone apps you can download to your son's phone that will disable it when he is behind the wheel.
◇ No talking on your cell phone, unless it's a parent calling. You may advise your son to pull off the road safely before he takes or returns your call.
◇ No other teens in the car. This is a smart rule for the first few months. But we believe that after your son has earned

your trust, you should allow him to drive one of his friends. Talk with him about whether he's able to stay focused on the road with his buddies in the car, though.

One of the reasons Dr. Barkley is such a proponent of limiting ADHD teens' nighttime driving is that accident rates spike late at night and early in the morning. If your son takes medication to manage his ADHD, you need to be aware of the times of the day that his medication begins to wear off. Take precautions to see that he avoids driving at those "trouble times." Here are other preventative measures you can take:

◇ If you can, provide your son with a big, slow car to drive.
◇ Figure out an "essential documents" system. He'll need to remember his driver's license and the registration and insurance card for whatever car he's driving. Together, devise a routine to help him remember these every time he drives. That will be easy if he always carries a wallet. If he doesn't, you may need to put together a "car backpack" that always goes with him in the car.
◇ Make sure he understands the long-term consequences of reckless driving. This includes death to himself or others, injury, property damage, and loss of his driver's license.
◇ Make sure your son knows what to do in case of emergency. Does he know how to handle an accident? A flat tire or other mechanical breakdown? Should he get in the car with a stranger who's pulled over to offer help? Does your family have a roadside assistance program? Go over the scenarios with him not to frighten him, but to help him be prepared.
◇ Consider having your son pay for his own auto insurance. The greater the risk he becomes, the more his insurance will cost. He'll have a financial incentive to stay safe.
◇ Sign a safe driver contract with your son. There are plenty of examples of these kinds of documents online, or you

can draft your own. In a typical contract, the teen agrees that he and all passengers will wear seatbelts, that he will obey all traffic laws, and that he will not drive under the influence of drugs or alcohol. You promise to give him calm and respectful feedback on his driving, and you agree not to punish him if he calls you for a ride home because he's under the influence of drugs or alcohol. Often, such an agreement also outlines who is responsible for various car-related expenses. Posting your contract in a prominent place will help a teen with ADHD remember what he agreed to do.

◇ Remember the "other stuff." We remember a story one mom told about her son, a new driver who had ADHD. The young man pulled into a service station to get gas. He put the nozzle into the tank and began to pump the fuel before deciding to run into the convenience store for a snack. He paid for his food, returned to his car, and sped off—forgetting all about the gasoline that was still pumping away. Help your young driver remember that he has to pay attention all the time, not just when he's behind the wheel.

◇ Set a good example for him. If you want him to drive safely, make sure he sees you driving safely. Your behavior, in this or any situation, will always have a powerful impact on your son.

Discipline That Works

Your teenage son is almost a grownup—but not yet. Just as many of the other parenting strategies have evolved, you also need to find discipline techniques that are appropriate and effective. Your new approach needs to respect your son's increasing maturity and preserve your relationship with him. And it needs to help you keep your home a peaceful place.

Tall order? Maybe. But you may have been juggling life with ADHD for a long time. You know that things are constantly evolving and changing. You can do this, too.

We can't possibly foresee every situation you might encounter. Instead, we'd like to outline a handful of discipline strategies we've observed. We'll tell you what tends to work and what doesn't, and you can "rent to own" them for yourself.

Natural Consequences

A lot of mainstream child psychologists suggest that a teenager be allowed to face the consequences of his own choices, without any intervention from his parents. If he neglects his homework, he'll fail his classes. If he annoys all of his classmates, he'll have no friends. If he can't remember to go to work, he'll get fired from his job. This may be effective in the general population, but boys with ADHD are much more easily discouraged. If he fails at any one of these things, he may convince himself that he'll never succeed at anything. Or, because his memory may be poor, he may not remember the consequences long enough for them to have the desired effect. He needs more encouragement and support than this form of discipline typically provides, particularly in more important matters like school performance.

Consistent, Mild Consequences

This tactic, we find, can be a more effective solution to chronic discipline problems for a boy with ADHD. Instead of seeking a harsh punishment, look for the least restrictive, most lenient punishment possible. Teenagers with ADHD remember one thing: That they were punished. They don't tend to remember how long they were punished. Lengthy punishments often end up hurting the entire family, without any additional benefit. Teens with ADHD often repeat the unacceptable behavior, even when they've been punished. You may have to take away your son's iPod or cell phone for 20 two-day periods over the course of a year, but eventually he'll get the point.

Grounding

It's rare for any teenager to escape getting grounded. But you need to proceed with caution if you're going to go down this road. Grounding your son will take him out of activities for a week, 2 weeks, a month—whatever sentence you've pronounced. That's a long time for a kid whose social network is already probably very fragile and whose social skills need daily practice. If you isolate him, the effects could range from rebellion to depression. If you must use this as a method of discipline, we recommend it only for short periods of time (a day or two). We also suggest that you warn your son ahead of time that this is the consequence he'll face for particular rule violations.

Losing Car or Telephone Privileges

Neither of these are given rights, though your teenager might be surprised to learn this. It's perfectly reasonable to refuse him the right to talk on the phone for a while if he runs up a monumental cell phone bill. You can also take the car keys for a week if he's chronically late getting home and it's become a major inconvenience. But don't take away the car for 2 months if his room is messy. That's an overreaction.

Negotiate

There should be room in your relationship for both of you to express your opinions about whatever you feel he did wrong. You both need to speak respectfully and calmly. For a boy with ADHD, this can be an empowering way to build conflict-resolution skills in a nonthreatening environment.

Second Chances

Far more than other kids, boys with ADHD need plenty of second (and third and fourth) chances to regain your trust and prove they have learned whatever lesson you've meant to teach. If your son messes up, by all means, discipline him. But after a while, give him another chance along with a hearty dose of forgiveness and encouragement.

Admit You Don't Know It All

By now, your son has you pretty well figured out. He knows you're not perfect. Why not admit it every once in awhile? When he makes a mistake, let him off the hook. Instead of punishing him, tell him about one of the dopey things you did when you were growing up, maybe something you never told your parents. You don't always have to be the enforcer.

The Last Word on the Last Word

Your son may argue every point. Some teens with ADHD do. It can be a tremendous source of stimulation for him and next to impossible for him to resist. But it's a no-win situation for you. Try not to let yourself get drawn into pointless arguments with your son. If you do, either let him have the last word or simply refuse to discuss the matter until he stops arguing.

You've spent a lifetime—your son's lifetime—helping him. Now you're in the strange and uneasy position of needing to pull back a little here, a lot there. How will you know when to stop helping? Well, one mom put it this way: "I'll stop when I'm no longer needed." Another one said, "Don't do something for your son that he can do for himself."

Your Son's Self-Esteem

The adolescent and teen years can be rough on any kid's self-confidence. As a boy grows into his man's body, he may experience moments of pure awkwardness he's sure no adult can comprehend. The girls around him seem so mature, so unapproachable. He may want to talk to those beautiful, foreign creatures—but how? His own body betrays him: His voice cracks, his arms and legs seem too long to control, his face breaks out. If only he could be taller, or shorter, or more athletic, or funnier, or have better hair. He's overflowing with emotions, but he doesn't have the inclination or the words to express them. So those feelings get stuffed inside, making him crazy.

And then factor in ADHD.

If your son has been struggling with his ADHD since he was a little boy, there's a chance his self-esteem may already have taken a hard hit. Many labels may have been attached to him over the years, and he may still carry the hurt from them. Just think of what he may have been called—or worse, what he may have called himself:

◊ lazy,
◊ disruptive,
◊ daydreamer,
◊ misbehaved,
◊ dumb, or
◊ unfocused.

Is it any wonder that by the time they're in their early teens, some boys find it impossible to list even one of their strengths? Certainly, that's a worst-case scenario. As a caring parent, you can take measures to restore or protect your son's self-confidence. In fact, it's essential that you do so. His self-esteem is closely linked to his likelihood for success now and into adulthood.

Components of Self-Esteem

An individual builds self-esteem bit by bit, by succeeding in life, at school, with friends, and in relationships. True positive self-worth, particularly in the case of a young person with ADHD, needs to include a number of elements:

◊ He believes he can identify and fix what's wrong. Your son already knows that life with ADHD is extra challenging. If his self-esteem is healthy, he has begun to develop the ability to identify when there's a problem and to have confidence that he can, with effort, work toward a solution. If his grades have slipped, he's aware of the steps he needs to take. If he's had an argument with a buddy, he doesn't give up on the friendship. He figures out what went wrong and works it out. The key to this aspect of self-esteem is his *belief* that his efforts will be productive.

◊ He tries. Many teens with ADHD have become the unwitting victims of "learned helplessness." It's often quicker and easier for adults to do something for a child with ADHD than it is to teach that child to do it for himself. Sadly, when that child grows up, he believes there are many things he's incapable of doing on his own. That can result in an extremely low sense of self-worth. On the other hand, a young man who's willing to take a risk and attempt to figure things out—even if he's not successful all of the time— is likely to have much higher self-esteem. He will believe that trying may result in success, at least sometimes.

◊ He views his ADHD not as a problem but as something that makes him different and special. Believing that you're unique is a key component to healthy self-esteem. As he grows older, your son may begin to see his ADHD as a sort of gift that sets him apart. Encourage this sort of thinking, and he'll feel good about who he is and how he's wired. Make sure he knows about the long list of influential, talented, and often brilliant people who have (or were believed to have had) ADHD, including Albert Einstein, Thomas Edison, Benjamin Franklin, Alexander Graham Bell, Abraham Lincoln, John F. Kennedy, Walt Disney, Henry Ford, Babe Ruth, Michael Jordan, Nolan Ryan, Michael Phelps, Pablo Picasso, Robin Williams, and Sylvester Stallone.

◇ He develops and maintains self-control. As he grows toward adulthood, your son needs to know that ADHD is not in charge of him. A person with high self-esteem is in command of himself, his feelings, and his reactions. Although this ability may be naturally delayed in a young man with ADHD, it's a crucial part of self-confidence to know that you can trust yourself to stay in control.

◇ He acknowledges his own efforts and rewards himself. If your son feels valued and confident, then he'll understand it's OK to give himself a pat on the back when he really tries hard at something. He might even buy himself a gift or do something fun to celebrate. If he's feeling good about himself, then he'll realize that it's the effort that earns the reward, nor the outcome. He's not after perfection, which is unhealthy. He's rewarding persistence, which is especially challenging for a boy with ADHD.

◇ He has a parent or parents who support him, praise him, and love him for who he is. Time and again, adults with ADHD report that their parents were their most consistent encouragers. As children and teens, they knew home was a safe place. They never doubted their self-worth, because they always felt loved by the people who mattered most in their lives. If you remember only one sentence from this book, remember this one: *The best predictor of success for a child with ADHD is having someone believe in him while he is growing up.* This finding comes from more than 15 years of research conducted by Dr. Gabrielle Weiss, coauthor of the 1993 book *Hyperactive Children Grown Up.*

So what does healthy self-esteem look like? In this case, that may be better answered by discussing what it doesn't look like. Your son shouldn't be walking around feeling inferior every day of his life. But it's also a warning sign if he constantly brags that he's better than everybody else. That kind of false bravado can be a red flag for real self-confidence trouble lurking beneath the surface of his big talk. Your son should know that he has strengths and weaknesses, that he's wonderfully flawed just like the rest of us. Like everything in your walk with ADHD, the pursuit of healthy self-esteem is about balance.

Self-Esteem and Motivation

You can see that a young man who feels positive about his efforts is much more likely to believe he can grow toward mastering skills, even the ones that have eluded him because of his ADHD.

Still, as you may have sensed, motivation itself can be a continuing challenge. An essential part of emotional maturity includes development of *internal motivation*. Internal motivation results when a young person no longer needs rewards or incentives to remain focused on a task and follow it through to completion. It's a kind of willpower that develops as we grow up. Boys with ADHD tend to struggle to achieve this kind of maturity and self-motivation.

You can also see how closely this can be tied in with a person's self-esteem. If your son believes he stands little or no chance of succeeding, he will have almost no motivation to apply himself, whether it's to a school project or to a relationship. His positive outlook is essential in helping him remain motivated, especially as he matures, and that motivation needs to come from within.

Young adulthood is an excellent time to introduce role models and historic figures who have found a way to shine despite their ADHD. A small child might not be able to identify with the work of Albert Einstein or Thomas Edison. But your teen can understand that our world would be vastly different if those two men hadn't ignored the critics who labeled them as problem students. Or perhaps there's an adult in your life who's carved his own niche despite an ADHD diagnosis. Many teens with ADHD thrive in one-on-one mentoring situations. The idea is for your son to gain valuable motivational tools from people who inspire him.

Self-Esteem Strategies for Teens

As your son matures, he becomes more capable of understanding how his own actions and thought patterns contribute to his self-esteem. Encourage him to boost his own self-esteem with strategies like the following:

◊ He can develop "islands of competence." This concept comes from Dr. Robert Brooks, educator and faculty member at Harvard Medical School. Everyone has some special gift, and some people have many. Your son needs to have at least one special area in which he can shine. It may be art, sports, music, computer programming, or electronics.

◊ Inventory the life skills that will serve him well as an adult. Ironically, the same qualities that are considered a drawback in a child with ADHD can be really beneficial to an adult in the workplace. It can be an eye-opening exercise to look at your son's individual characteristics and define which ones might be extremely valuable to him later in life. For example, his high energy level is frustrating when he's expected to sit still all day in school. But it will serve him very well if he decides to pursue a career in sales. Challenge him to brainstorm ways his gifts will help him in the future. You might also arrange to have him take an online inventory (like the Keirsey Temperament Sorter or the Myers-Briggs Type Indicator) to help him determine his skills and personality strengths.

◇ Good is great. In many, many cases, boys with ADHD aren't striving to be the stars of the team or take home the blue ribbons. They just want to know they're good. This is really healthy thinking. Knowing he's good in at least one area will help him realize he can be good at many other things.

◇ Set small goals. It can be self-defeating to look at an overwhelming challenge, particularly for a kid with ADHD. It's far gentler on the self-confidence to set smaller goals and feel the confidence boost that comes from achieving each one. Imagine your son thinking about saving enough money to buy a car. Now help him break that down into small, manageable pieces: $25 a month, for instance. Maybe you'll even match all (or a portion) of it if he's faithful to his goal. By overcoming the challenge bit by bit, his confidence will build and he'll see he *can* do it.

◇ Have hope. Things tend to happen just a little later for people with ADHD. Encourage him not to lose sight of the fact that good things will still happen for him, even if he feels like ADHD has really messed up his life. Keeping a "gratitude journal" might not be right up his alley, but it doesn't hurt a guy's self-esteem to talk from time to time about the things that are going right. Sometimes we forget about them.

Strategies for Parents

Your teenaged son comes into contact with a lot of people, directly or indirectly—friends, teammates, teachers, coaches, and

TV and movie characters. However, don't for a minute forget the influence *you* continue to have in building and nurturing his feelings of self-worth.

◊ Love him unconditionally. Love your son exactly as he is—his gifts, his talents, his quirks, his faults. His self-esteem depends upon knowing he's precious to you, not a bother, despite the wild ride his ADHD sometimes puts you through.

◊ Make a list of his strengths. Begin to list all of your son's gifts and talents. Once you get going, it's hard to stop. Find a quiet time to share your list with him, and make sure he has a copy of it. It may become one of his most cherished possessions. And after you've made the list . . .

◊ Help him build on those strengths. As a parent of a young man with ADHD, you need to keep him engaged and growing. Once his eyes have been opened to his many gifts, explore together how he can build upon them. Find seminars he can attend, books he can read, and volunteering or job-shadowing opportunities he can pursue.

◊ Have fun with him. Make sure to laugh together. Enjoy each other. Create memories.

◊ Stay engaged. As your son matures, continue teaching him the skills he needs to feel confident in life. He's old enough now to really grasp the consequences of his actions on himself and others, and you can coach him. For instance, helping him with anger management will keep him from destroying his own possessions (self) and alienating his friends (others). Continued work on time management will keep him from missing activities (self) and rudely keeping people waiting (others). Self-esteem stems from mastery of these kinds of skills.

◊ Teach by example. You cannot simply bestow self-esteem upon someone. You need to demonstrate how your choices and actions produce your own feelings of self-worth. Show your son where your self-esteem comes from.

◊ Praise him. But do so genuinely. Like all kids, your son has a finely tuned "fake praise" meter. He'll know when he deserves praise and when he doesn't. If you gush with praise over trivial things, your true admiration will become meaningless. (And remember to praise effort, not outcome.)

◊ Don't let your fears become his fears. Many parents of boys with ADHD develop a "worst-case" mindset. They end up envisioning the darkest possible future for their sons. Most children are very perceptive. Watch the words you use, your tone of voice, the looks you give. You can tell him a lot without ever saying a word.

◊ Listen when he speaks. Especially for a boy, this may not happen often. He needs to know you're willing to put down what you're doing, look him in the eye, and hear what he has to say without interrupting him. Problem-solve with him, and look for win-win solutions. Involve him in decisions. This goes a long way toward making him feel valued.

Remember, the most effective support he'll ever get comes from you, when you say and believe with your whole heart, "I know you can do it." He is ready, or he will be. You have to think of your son as a whole, independent, capable person.

You've spent a lifetime—your son's lifetime—helping him. Now you're in the strange and uneasy position of needing to pull back a little here, a lot there. How will you know when to stop helping? Well, one mom puts it this way: "I'll stop helping when I'm no longer needed."

Points to Consider

1. Remember to nurture the relationship you have with your son. Nearly everything else is secondary.

2. There are no careers a person with ADHD can't pursue, and no jobs a person with ADHD can't do. Remind your child he has what it takes to succeed in any area he's passionate about, gifted in, and dedicated to.

3. If your son has struggled with ADHD since he was a little boy, he may have been called a lot of hurtful names:
    ◊ lazy,
    ◊ disruptive,
    ◊ poorly behaved,
    ◊ stupid, or
    ◊ unfocused.

4. Be very, very cautious how you speak to and about your son, and what your expressions and body language say to him. He needs to know you see his value. Children who do best in overcoming the challenges of ADHD are the ones who can say, "Somebody believes in me." Don't you want to be that person for your son?

Action Steps to Take Now

1. Set reasonable expectations for your son's performance at school, at home, and in the community, and require him to live up to his end of the bargain. He is not a child.

2. Together with your son, explore sports, clubs, activities, volunteer work, and part-time job opportunities that are interesting and appealing to him.

3. Buy or borrow a copy of *25 Ways to Win With People* by Drs. John C. Maxwell and Les Parrott. Involve the whole family in reading and reviewing its principles.

4. Be sure you understand the significance of your son's ADHD as it relates to issues of sexuality and impulse control. Have open and honest discussions with him about dating.

5. Consider carefully your son's readiness to drive. When he does get his license, consider implementing a graduated driving system while he gains experience and builds confidence.

6. Make sure your son knows his strengths. This is an essential step toward regaining or reinforcing his self-esteem.

7. Praise your son when he tries, listen when he speaks, and love him all of the time.

Chapter 6

When More Support Is Needed

Sometimes even your most effective parenting tools and your son's best efforts are not enough to enable him to succeed in the classroom without interventions. Could your son use additional time on tests, frequent cueing to stay focused, or a behavior plan? If so, how do you go about advocating for your son? We tell our clients that learning information about accommodations and services the school can provide is critical. If your son's ADHD significantly impacts his life at school, the following federal laws could enable him to receive assistance if he meets the qualifications:

◊ Section 504 of the Rehabilitation Act of 1973 (referred to as Section 504) and its companion federal laws—American with Disabilities Act (ADA) and Americans with Disabilities Amendments Act of 2008 (ADAAA); and

◊ Individuals with Disabilities Educational Improvement Act of 2004 (called IDEA), which began as Public Law

94–142, the Education of All Handicapped Children's Act in 1975, and has been amended multiple times.

Sometimes the school will initiate the process for services and accommodations. Often, however, parents need to take the leadership role. In cases where you have to initiate and drive the process, it will be important for you to understand the parameters of both Section 504 and IDEA to help you determine which best fits your son's needs. The following sections give you the information you will need to have a basic understanding of both 504 and IDEA.

What Is Section 504?

Section 504 is a federal civil rights law that protects children with disabilities from ages 3–21 against discrimination in public and nonreligious schools, including colleges and technical schools receiving federal funds. However, it does not provide funding; it simply mandates accommodations and some services. The intent is to provide a level playing field so the student's disability will not interfere with his access to education. Section 504 states:

> No qualified individual with a disability shall, on the basis of disability, be excluded from participation in or be denied the benefits of the services, programs or activities of a public entity, or be subjected to discrimination by any public entity. (35.130, Subpart B, p. 549)

According to the Americans with Disabilities Act of 1990 (ADA),
The term "disability" means, with respect to an individual—
A. has a physical or mental impairment that substantially limits one or more major life activities
B. has a record of such impairment
C. regarded as having such impairment. (HR 3195 RH)

Your son could meet items B or C above and be guaranteed freedom from discrimination, but he would *not* be eligible for services and accommodations under a 504 Plan *unless* he had met the first requirement—"a physical or mental impairment that *substantially limits* one or more major life activities." In essence, your child can be diagnosed with ADHD by an outside source or can be suspected of having ADHD but still not be determined eligible for accommodations through a 504 plan because he demonstrates no substantial impairment in the school setting. A team of personnel from the school, which isn't tightly defined by 504 and doesn't always include parents, must determine if the ADHD *substantially limits* your child's access to an education on a case-by-case basis.

The impact of American with Disabilities Act Amendments Act of 2008 (ADAAA) included the following changes:

◊ the definition of "disability" under Section 504 was broadened to include "learning, reading, concentrating, thinking, communicating, and working" (Section 2A);

◊ it clarified that an impairment could limit one major activity but not others and could be episodic;

◊ it stated effects of medication and other forms of assistance should not be considered when determining if an impairment substantially limits a major activity (that means that if your son is receiving medication, the team should consider what his performance would be like without the medication. Why? If those supports were withdrawn, your son's performance might decline significantly); and

◊ broad interpretation is given to the term "substantially limits."

What Does the 504 Process Look Like?

Most schools will follow similar steps to these to determine if you son is eligible under Section 504:

1. The school will gather information about your son's classroom performance, which might include teacher observations, grades, results of standardized assessments, and any outside medical or psychological information you might provide.

2. The school team may or may not require additional evaluation. As a parent, you have the right to request an evaluation of your child through the school district. Once permission is signed for the evaluation, it must be completed within 60 school days.

3. An eligibility determination will be made by the 504 team. If the team determines that your son's ADHD substantially limits his academic performance or behavior at school, it would determine him eligible for a formal 504 plan.

4. A written 504 plan will be developed to delineate services and accommodations. It is reviewed annually but can be revisited at any time and is kept in place as long as needed. Even though a 504 plan includes strategies and assistance that an effective teacher would normally implement, it is always important to have it in writing. Without it, one year you may have a teacher who makes accommodations, and the next year you may have one who does not. Going forward, you want to ensure your son has the accommodations he needs and that they are provided consistently from classroom to classroom.

Jim's son has a 504 plan for his ADHD that was established at the end of his kindergarten year. Jim and his wife had Teddy privately evaluated by a psychologist and brought the paperwork to school. After reviewing the report, the school met with the Forgans and determined Teddy was eligible for a 504 plan. Because Teddy was struggling, there was no resistance from the school toward writing the 504 plan, and Jim and his wife were pleased with the accommodations. Some of the accommodations written on his first-grade 504 plan included not taking away all of his recess, allowing reduced homework, providing spelling words on Friday instead of Monday, and allowing frequent breaks.

What Is IDEA?

IDEA is the federal law that states that a free and appropriate education must be provided to all students who have a disability, meet their state's eligibility criteria, and have an *educational need* for special education services. IDEA provides funding for instruction, addressing your child's unique needs, usually from a special education teacher, and can provide related services like occupational therapy or counseling when needed. The federal law specifies 13 disability categories. Other Health Impairment (OHI) is the eligibility category most often considered for children with ADHD. Other disability categories could be considered, depending on your son's specific difficulties. If he has academic problems, he may qualify under Specific Learning Disabilities. If your son has serious behavioral or emotional problems, he may qualify under Emotional Behavioral Disorder.

If a child is considered for services under the Other Health Impairment eligibility, he must have a disability (such as ADHD) that significantly impacts his ability to learn and perform in the classroom to the extent that he would require special education services. Factors other than his test scores should be considered. Those factors might include "grades, homework completion, independent work habits, alertness, sleeping in class, class participation and attendance, ability to complete schoolwork and tests within specified time frames, relationships with peers, and compliance with rules" (Durheim & Zeigler Dendy, 2006, p. 128).

How Is the Disability Category OHI Defined Under IDEA?

Federal law defines OHI as

> having limited strength, vitality or alertness, including a heightened alertness to environmental stimuli, that results in limited alertness with respect to the educational environment, that:
>
> A. Is due to chronic or acute health problems such as asthma, attention deficit disorder, or attention deficit hyperactivity disorder, diabetes, epilepsy, a heart condition, hemophilia, lead poisoning, leukemia, nephritis, rheumatic fever, and sickle cell anemia; and
>
> B. Adversely affects a child's educational performance. (IDEA, 2004, Section 300.8(c)(9))

If your son qualifies as having a disability under IDEA, then the school staff meets with you to write an Individualized Education Program (IEP). IDEA requires that your child must be educated in the least restrictive environment (LRE), meaning that he must be educated in a general education classroom setting as much as possible. Schools have different options for delivering educational services. Many have inclusion classrooms where a special education teacher comes into the classroom for part of the day or the general education teacher is trained in techniques for instructing children with disabilities. Elsewhere, the child leaves the general education classroom for a portion of the day to receive instruction in areas where he needs extra help. We recommend http://www.SeeMyIEP. com as a website where you can obtain real IEP advice and see real IEP goals.

What Would the IDEA Process Look Like?

The school may follow steps similar to these in determining if your child qualifies under IDEA:

1. The school would gather information about your son's classroom performance, which might include teacher observations, grades, results of standardized assessments, and any outside medical or psychological information you might provide.

2. A formal evaluation is required, either done through the school district or provided by you from an acceptable outside source or a combination of the above. As a parent, you have the right to request an evaluation of your child. Once permission is signed for the evaluation, it must be completed within 60 school days.

3. An eligibility determination will be made by the IEP team. If the team determines that your son's ADHD is a disability that requires special education services, then it would determine him eligible for a disability category.

4. A written IEP would be developed to delineate services and accommodations. It is reviewed annually and a reevaluation is considered every 3 years.

How Are 504 and IDEA Different?

Generally, children who qualify for IDEA are more impaired and require more services than those best served by a 504 plan. IDEA provides actual funding to schools for special education instruction specified in an IEP, while a 504 plan provides no additional funding to schools but affords your son accommodations and some services such as a quiet place to work, use of educational aids such as computers, or small-group instruction. As you would expect, the qualification procedure is less stringent for Section 504.

IDEA requires the development of an IEP that specifies the student's current levels of performance, specific goals written for a year in all areas where he is below his grade level peers (with specification about how these goals will be monitored), and details about where and for how long special education services will be provided. A 504 plan requires only written documentation of accommodations.

Members of the IEP team under IDEA are specified by law and must include the parents; a teacher knowledgeable about the child; a special education teacher; an administrator (usually called a Local Education Authority or LEA), who is knowledgeable about the laws, disabilities, and general curriculum; and someone who can interpret test results such as a school psychologist or speech and language pathologist. Members of the 504 team are not as clearly defined.

IDEA requires a formalized evaluation that might include a psychoeducational evaluation of the child's intelligence, academic levels, and processing abilities and possibly behavior rating scales. It could require a medical diagnosis of ADHD. Eligibility criteria can vary by school districts. 504 requires some documentation of the child's difficulties, but it could include results of rating scales, teacher and parent information, and medical information.

IDEA requires consideration of reevaluation needs every 3 years. Many times those reevaluations might be results of assessments and written observations provided by the classroom teacher. If your son has a 504 plan, it does not have a specific 3-year reevaluation component.

More specific parental rights come into play with IDEA, such as clearly defined due process rights when there is a serious disagreement between the school district and the parents over the need for an evaluation or determination of services. Section 504 provides for parent rights, usually left up to the discretion of local school districts, which are not as extensive but still allow parents to contest a 504 determination.

Paperwork required in IDEA is more stringent and requires specific written notice of eligibility or ineligibility. Under IDEA, an official IEP meeting is required before any change in placement can occur. The 504 requires no such meeting. Table 5 further outlines the differences between the two laws.

How Are 504 and IDEA Alike?

Both are based on federal laws requiring that a child with a disability receive a free and appropriate public education (FAPE). As we've said earlier, the laws attempt to level the playing field so your son will have the same access to education as his nondisabled peers. For example, if he processes information slowly or loses his focus so frequently that he can't finish his work in a specified amount of time, he may be given extended time to complete his work.

Both can provide accommodations such as extended time to complete work, lessons broken down into smaller segments or "chunked," and copies of notes provided for the student's use.

Both require a formal eligibility process with paperwork that must be kept confidential. This allows the teacher and those working with the child to have knowledge of his disability and the required accommodations. Each plan requires an annual review, although parents can request a review at any time.

Both laws require that the child be educated in the least restrictive environment with nondisabled peers as much as possible. Both eligibilities transfer if your child moves to a different school, but they may have to be rewritten.

Due process rights are provided by both laws when a parent disagrees with a school district over a child being eligible or services provided. The due process in IDEA is specified by federal law, whereas the due process in section 504 is left up to the local school district. The similarities between IDEA and Section 504 are further summarized in Figure 7.

Table 5

How IDEA and Section 504 Differ

IDEA	504
Office of Special Education of the U.S. Department of Education responsible for enforcement	Office for Civil Rights of the U.S. Department of Education responsible for enforcement
Students generally more impaired and require more service	Students generally don't require special instruction
Funding provided based on disability category	No funding provided to schools, but schools receiving IDEA funds must meet 504 requirements
More stringent qualification procedure	Less stringent qualification procedure
Individualized Education Plan (IEP) developed	504 plan written
Members of IEP team specified by law	504 team may vary by school district
Formal evaluation necessary	Some documentation of difficulties necessary
Reevaluation to be considered every 3 years	No reevaluation specified
More specific parental rights	Parent rights provided but not as stringent as IDEA
Official IEP meeting and parent permission required before change in placement can occur	No meeting required, but parent should be informed

What Determines Which Is Most Appropriate for My Son?

The decision will be based on the needs of your son and the extent of his impairment. If he needs individualized instruction from a special education teacher, eligibility under IDEA should be considered. Remember that if your son is eligible for special education, the goal will be to have him remain in a general classroom as

---

How are IDEA and Section 504 alike?
- Both are federal laws requiring FAPE.
- Both have accommodations and some services available.
- A formal eligibility process is required for both.
- Paperwork for both laws must be kept confidential.
- Under both laws, the child is to be educated in the least restrictive environment with his nondisabled peers as much as possible.
- Eligibilities under both laws transfer from school to school but may have to be rewritten.
- Under both laws, due process rights are provided when a parent disagrees with the school district.

Figure 7. Similarities between IDEA and Section 504.

---

much as possible. With an eligibility under IDEA, he could also access other services as needed such as occupational or language therapy.

Boys with ADHD often may be eligible under multiple categories. For example, a comprehensive evaluation may determine that he has a specific learning disability or an emotional and behavioral disorder. If so, his IEP would address those issues.

On the other hand, if your son is doing relatively well, he may only need accommodations in the classroom, such as being reminded to pay attention, permissible movement, or extended time, so his needs could be met through a 504 plan.

What Can Parents Do?

◊ Try to maintain good communication with your son's teacher(s).

◊ Advocate for your son and make sure the 504 or IEP (IDEA) team has a clear picture of your son and his struggles.

◊ Provide any outside documentation that might help the team.

◊ Request an evaluation if more information is needed. Put your request in writing and keep a copy.

◇   Try to understand the eligibility process and parental rights for your school district, often addressed on their website, and make yourself an integral part of the team by doing what you can do to help your son. Some parents bring advocates or attorneys to the table, but Mary Anne's experience as a school psychologist has been that this is usually unnecessary. Check with your school district to determine if parent liaisons are available to assist with problem solving and support. As a parent, you have the option to request mediation or a due process hearing if you and the school cannot agree on what your son needs.

What if I Don't Want to Label My Child?

Some parents are reluctant to create a "paper trail" and formalize their child's disability in the school's records, but it is better for your son's chronic problems to be understood for what they are—deficits in neurocognitive processes that affect his day-to-day functioning. It's not laziness, lack of ability, or obstinacy. At times, early intervention provided through accommodations on a 504 plan could prevent the need for special education services later. The goal of a 504 plan or IDEA eligibility is not to provide a crutch or an easy out for your son but to enable him to receive the support he needs to be as successful as possible when he's at school.

When we worked with Jeremy, he was constantly in trouble in his first-grade classroom. His performance was falling further and further behind that of his peers. Jeremy was not completing his work, was making careless errors, and didn't seem to be able to answer simple comprehension questions about stories he had read. The school implemented a Response to Intervention (RtI) plan targeting specific reading skills, one of the first steps in most states to look at whether a child has a learning disability. His RtI plan involved small-group instruction by the classroom teacher in comprehension. His progress was monitored weekly over a 6–8 week period. With the additional assistance on reading, he showed improvement.

Because Jeremy seemed to be making progress, the school did not pursue formalized testing to determine if he had a learning disability. However, he was still having difficulty staying in his seat, doing his best work, and finishing assignments. We asked his parents and teachers to complete rating scales that assessed Jeremy's functioning as compared with other children his age. Those ratings showed significantly more inattentive and disorganized behaviors than would be expected given his age, so the school initiated a meeting to discuss his eligibility for a 504 plan. His parents brought in documentation of his ADHD diagnosis (not required but helpful), and the team developed a 504 plan. It included an individualized task-monitoring plan, which his teacher used to help Jeremy keep track of his responsibilities. He received a check for each item completed and turned in, for checking his work, and for self-monitoring his reading. He was able to earn special privileges, such as additional time on the computer, with the check marks he received. In addition, he received frequent cueing on tasks by his teacher and opportunities to move about the classroom to different stations when his work was completed. He showed progress and benefited from the provisions of his 504 plan.

The Importance of Establishing Eligibility Before College

Many students benefit from the structure provided at home and the efforts of elementary and secondary school faculties. When they get to college, they sometimes fall apart without those supports. If you suspect your son's ADHD might cause him significant difficulty in college, it is important to establish eligibility for 504 or IDEA before he leaves secondary school, so his needs and accommodations will already be documented. The eligibilities don't transfer to the college setting, but the paper trail can be helpful.

Postsecondary institutions do provide accommodations and services but may require more information such as updated testing. Requirements for receiving accommodations on the SAT and ACT for students with ADHD have become more stringent in recent years. In addition to a diagnosis, the student must provide a comprehensive evaluation that is not more than 3 years old and was completed by a licensed professional.

Classroom Accommodations and Supports

As your son's advocate, you should be familiar with the universe of options that could be available to your son. Listed on the following pages are examples of some of the accommodations that can be made with either a 504 plan or an IEP (take note that it is not an all-inclusive list). It is important to be realistic about what a teacher can be expected to do for your child and still manage an entire classroom. The best advice is to focus on the accommodations that you feel would be most beneficial to your son. The quality of the accommodations will likely be more effective than the quantity of interventions.

Classroom Structure
◊ Warnings provided before transitions. For example, the teacher gives your son a 5-minute warning before he must put away his work and begin a new task. It is helpful for some children to be allowed to begin cleaning up a few minutes before the rest of the class, allowing extra time to improve organizational skills.
◊ Placement of your child's desk in an area that is as free of distraction as possible. For example, you wouldn't want

your child's desk in an area where other students are constantly walking past it.

◊ A clean and clutter-free workspace to avoid distractions.

◊ Provision of a quiet workspace, such as a study carrel or quiet corner of the room, where your son could take his work.

◊ Placement near a positive role model.

◊ Scheduling accommodations. If there is an option, schedule more demanding classes earlier in the day and try to include some activity, such as physical education or recess, during the middle of the day.

◊ A specified place for turning in homework.

◊ Permissible movement such as allowing your son to get out of his desk and go to another area of the classroom for a specific purpose—to get materials or a drink of water or to run an errand for the teacher. Gaining the self-discipline not to bother other children would be important.

◊ Permission to stand beside his desk and work.

◊ Specific classroom routines and structure such as a specific routine for turning in homework.

◊ Establishing eye contact with the student when providing important information.

◊ Ignoring slight movement behaviors, like twirling a pencil, that do not interfere with classroom instruction.

Assignments

◊ Reduction in the amount of work to be completed. For example, in math, your son would complete the even-numbered problems rather than doing all of the problems.

◊ Assignments presented in manageable chunks. Your son could be given an assignment in several different parts so he isn't overwhelmed by the amount of work.

◊ Masking his papers. In this strategy, the student is encouraged to use a plain sheet of paper to cover up a portion of the page he is working on. This helps minimize the distraction from so much information on a page.

◊ Assistance in breaking down large assignments into manageable chunks.

◊ A monitoring plan to check work for careless mistakes before submitting it for grading.

◊ Positive reinforcement when grading papers, such as marking correct responses rather than wrong answers, if that would be more motivating to your son.

◊ Use of highlighter for key words in reading or mathematical signs.

◊ Frequent checks to ensure that the student has understood directions. Sometimes it may be helpful for your son to repeat directions to the teacher.

◊ Watching for signs that the student does not understand the assignment and providing additional instruction.

◊ An example of what the finished product should look like.

◊ Multimodal instructions—visual and auditory instructions paired with hands-on learning when possible.

◊ Use of technology such as computer programs—often an effective way for a boy with ADHD to practice skills.

◊ Study guides in writing when possible, as well as copies of notes or board work.

◊ Access to word processing programs on computers to produce written work.

Self-Regulatory Skills

◊ Training in turn-taking, waiting in line, remaining seated, and identifying cause and effect, especially important in kindergarten and first grade.

◊ Opportunities to regain self-control by removing himself from overwhelming situations.

◊ Holding "stress" balls or fidget toys in his hands, especially if they enhance concentration.

◊ Assistance in organizational strategies such as writing items in an agenda and keeping papers in their proper place.

◊ Opportunities to self-manage behavior. For example, your son counts and records a specific behavior with teacher assistance and receives positive, corrective feedback and some reward such as verbal praise or a tangible item.

◊ Placement on an individualized behavior management plan where the teacher monitors behavior in specific areas and your son earns rewards such as additional computer time, lunch with the teacher or a special friend, or tokens. These are most effective when the system carries over to the home and parents are reinforcing the same behaviors.

Memory

◊ Frequent repetition and review of previously learned material.

◊ Provision of cue cards that would outline steps, especially important in solving math problems requiring sequential steps like long division.

◊ Use of a calculator.

◊ Assistance in attaching new learning to previously learned material.

◊ Use of memory techniques such as mnemonics.

◊ Overlearning until it becomes firmly embedded in long-term memory. This may require intensive practice, repetition, and review.

◊ Assistance in organizing information into meaningful categories.

◊ Assistance in using verbal rehearsal (repeating information to himself) or using visual imagery to assist with recall.

During his school-age years, Mary Anne's son never required a 504 plan or special education eligibility. There were times he could have benefited from some accommodations, such as being allowed to make up tests he had missed in a quiet environment or receiving extended time on complex testing, but his strong self-regulation skills helped him do well. His organization skills improved over time, and even though it was often a scramble at the end, he was always able to produce projects on time. Mary Anne made sure he had a quiet place to work and tools that he needed, and encouraged him to break large assignments into manageable components well ahead of the due date. However, he seemed to work more effectively under the pressure of time. The summer prior to his senior year in high school, Mary Anne was conducting a college preparatory camp where he had ample time to write his college essays. However, true to form, he generally completed each one the night before he mailed the application. Once attending college, he found the academic demands were much greater than in high school, and he needed the accommodation of extended time on classroom tests. This process was not too difficult to accomplish.

When the Current School Setting Isn't Working

In some cases, boys with ADHD cannot function in a public school with special education eligibility or 504 accommodations or in a private school providing some support. Other alternatives can include a special day or private school specializing in ADHD, learning disabilities, behavioral difficulties, or all three; specialized boarding schools; homeschooling; or virtual school. All of these options will require extensive research.

Homeschooling

Homeschooling is legal in all 50 states, so if you are interested in your state's specific requirements, contact your state Department of Education or check with your local school district. Homeschooling may be an option if a parent can commit the time, patience, and knowledge. It would require registering with your local school district; if it is large enough, it may have a separate office to handle homeschooling. There, you would be informed about state requirements, which usually entail annual evaluations to assess progress.

We believe that homeschooling is a viable choice for boys with ADHD and have recommended this option to some of our families. There are many considerations you must establish, including a structured and comprehensive curriculum, adequate supervision, and social opportunities with peers. Although we recognize that homeschooling is not for everyone, it works for many. Homeschooling provides parents the ability to give their son an individualized curriculum, no homework, opportunities for hands-on learning, and the possibility for him to be more active. In Jim's personal experience, homeschooling can allow your son to gain academic confidence and build his self-esteem. Some of our families homeschool their sons because it presents flexibility and does not require participation in high-stakes testing.

It is a myth that homeschooling is isolating and does not allow your son to have social interactions. Many communities have homeschool cooperatives (or co-ops) that you can join. There are also national, state, local, and online homeschool groups for you to investigate. Homeschooling affords your son the flexibility to interact with others as little or as much as you wish. Our advice is to ignore the naysayer that makes statements like, "He won't have any friends," "You'll feel alone," or "Homeschooling doesn't work for boys with ADHD." Jim knows firsthand that homeschooling can and does work for many boys with ADHD.

Our belief is that the homeschool movement will continue to expand and more resources will become available to support homeschooled boys with ADHD. These supports will include stronger curriculums, improved approaches to teach executive functioning skills, and educational options. One example of a homeschool option is an innovative homeschool center where Jim's son currently attends seventh grade.

At the end of fifth grade, Jim and his wife explored Teddy's educational options and decided that a homeschool program would best suit his middle school needs. Because Jim and his wife both work full-time in the education field, a homeschool center fit their circumstances far better than trying to have Teddy complete his homeschool lessons at home. They chose a learning center founded by Cindy Knoess, which partners with parents to facilitate and house instruction, monitor student progress, and mentor both the parent and the homeschooled student. A unique feature of the center they chose is that it is parent-directed but teacher-driven.

Parents enroll their student as a homeschool student in the traditional manner. With Cindy's help, parents select their son's academic curriculum. Most students attend the center Monday through Thursday; each works on his specific curriculum and is taught by certified teachers. There are a maximum of six students to one teacher, and students have a daily rotation through their subjects. Fridays are designated for field trips, community service activities, or as an optional instructional day at the center. Jim and his wife have been very satisfied with Teddy's progress and recommend a homeschool center as an option for boys with ADHD. Below is Jim's interview with Cindy regarding boys with ADHD and homeschooling.

> *Jim*: In your experiences managing a homeschool center, does homeschooling work for boys with ADHD?
>
> *Cindy*: Yes, I strongly believe that homeschooling is advantageous for the boy with ADHD. A homeschool center like mine works for boys with ADHD, but to be successful such a group-learning environment must be both highly structured and flexible. Not all homeschool groups offer both. Having parents and teachers experienced in working

with ADHD students is vital. The reasons I believe that a homeschool center works for boys with ADHD are:

◊ small groups of 4–5 students minimize distractions and provide high accountability;

◊ instruction and curriculum is matched to learning styles, which will usually be hands-on;

◊ discussion-based instruction is emphasized;

◊ multimedia is used frequently;

◊ a structured but flexible environment is created where boys can stand or pace while they work;

◊ frequent breaks and movement are allowed;

◊ homework is tailored to meet the unique needs of the student as they relate to the family; and

◊ a conducive environment for social skill development is present with direct teaching of study, organizational, and social skills that are difficult for parents to manage without the support of the other adults and instructors in the life of a student with ADHD.

Jim: What questions should a mom and/or dad ask themselves when considering homeschooling for a son with ADHD?

Cindy:

◊ Can I be consistent in teaching him regardless of the resistance I may encounter? A boy with ADHD is persistent; his energy can be exhausting. A parent must ask if he or she has the will to insist on follow-through time and time again.

◊ Do I truly understand the needs of a boy with ADHD, and am I prepared to plan for those needs? A boy with ADHD will need frequent changes in activities, but those transitions require guidance and minimal distractions to be beneficial. Planning the day so the boy with ADHD is engaged in frequent activities takes much effort.

◊ Am I prepared to change my thinking about traditional learning and think outside the box? I vividly remember a story told by a man diagnosed with ADHD who, at the time I heard him speak, was a professor at a local private university. He told of his father sitting outside in a chair reading aloud to him each day while he was climbing trees and playing. This man shared that long before ADHD was well-known, his dad instinctively knew that his son could learn while he was being active.

◊ Do I have the patience needed and the discernment required to support my son with ADHD as he struggles with his inattentiveness? A parent needs to be wise in knowing when it is good to push and when it is time to step back.

◊ Have I been forthcoming with my son about his ADHD? Does he understand it as well as I do? Does he view it as a medical condition that is not his fault—that his struggles are not because he is dumb or stupid or lacking intellectually?

◊ Do I understand how to tap into my son's strengths? Does he understand how to utilize his strengths? Many times this means the boy with ADHD excels in some kind of sport, especially outdoor recreational sports like hunting, archery, etc. Does the homeschool parent understand that it is vital to introduce his or her son to as many activities as possible so that he can develop interests and strengths outside of academics?

◊ Am I prepared to explore the community and the world outside of the classroom so that my son can learn from his experiences, as he is more likely to remember these lessons and to enjoy them more?

Jim: Are there specific steps a mom or dad should take when choosing a homeschool curriculum?

Cindy: Look for curriculum that presents information in small bites, so to speak. Frequent small lessons are perceived by your son as doable, as they will not seem to take so much concentration. There are some subjects that I recommend care in choosing texts that are not too "busy." For example, math is a subject where too many graphics and pictures can be distracting for the boy with ADHD and can contribute to the overall time a student will need to complete the work. Grammar is another subject area where less is better. To choose curriculum:

◊ First determine your son's ability level in each subject area, and choose a curriculum that is appropriately challenging.

◊ Look for meaningful content with simple presentation for challenging subject areas such as math and grammar.

◊ Select curriculum that presents material in small chunks with frequent assessments.

◊ Seek out curriculum that has multimedia components, as these can be engaging for boys with ADHD.

◊ Incorporate websites and software that enhance learning, such as Gizmos, BrainPop, the Learning A–Z sites, Kidspiration, Inspiration, etc.

◊ Check out programs created with boys in mind, such as the Institute for Excellence in Writing program, Handwriting Without Tears, the LEGO

Mindstorms engineering programs, and the Creation Studies Institute science curriculum.

In some cases, parents choose to provide the instruction for their son rather than use a homeschooling center. Although it is beyond the scope of this book to discuss specific curriculum choices, parents can choose between traditional, online, or virtual school homeschool experiences. When you're deciding, look for key features that include the quality of instructor resources for you, the types of hands-on activities offered for your son, the availability of computer-aided instruction, and the quality of the tracking system for recording your son's progress.

Of course, a prime secret for a successful homeschooling experience is having a good working relationship between the homeschooling parent and son. We use the term working relationship to emphasize that your son must be able and willing to complete schoolwork for you, the homeschool parent. You should have good organizational skills and the time to plan your instruction. We understand it is a full-time job to adequately homeschool your son and that parents benefit from the support of networking with other parents who are also homeschooling their sons with ADHD. Figure 8 includes our pros and cons of homeschooling a boy with ADHD.

You can weigh the pros and cons of homeschooling your son by creating your own chart. Check resources in your community and determine if there are homeschool centers or co-ops nearby. We have seen homeschooling work and understand it can be a viable option for boys with ADHD.

Virtual School

Many school districts offer virtual schools, in which students access courses online. Students have some interaction with a teacher but do the majority of their work on the computer. Some students

Pros	Cons
Customized curriculum	Parent as teacher (typically)
Online curriculum options	No paycheck for teaching your son
Flexibility	Patience required
Shortened school day	High structure necessary
Can work at a slower or faster pace	Difficult to stay disciplined and make progress
Increased opportunity for hands-on projects	Fewer social opportunities
Opportunity for movement	Dealing with his academic frustrations
No high-stakes state testing	Slower work speed means learning takes longer
Teach to his learning style	Reduced freedom for the teaching parent
No homework	High burnout rate
Freedom to teach your religious beliefs	Requires teaching multiple subjects
Opportunity to teach more real-life skills	Record keeping required to monitor progress
Support of other homeschool parents	Can't take advantage of benefits of public school (e.g., intensive tutoring, teacher expertise)

Figure 8. Pros and cons of homeschooling.

with ADHD are successful with computerized instruction because it can be faster paced than traditional classroom instruction, and much of the monotonous repetition can be eliminated. It is usually more effective with children in the upper elementary grades, middle school, and secondary students. Attending a virtual school requires consistent parental supervision and access to a computer with Internet access. Contact your local school district for more information.

Specialized Day Schools

For some families, there comes a point when their son's academic and/or behavioral difficulties approach the disaster level. Your son's ADHD may be so severe that he needs more than you or his current school can offer. His behavior may have escalated to the point that you don't know what to do for him, and you may be concerned for his safety and that of your family. He may be taking up the majority of your time and energy. Other family members may feel resentment or jealousy because of all of the time you spend on your son. This includes your time thinking and worrying about your son, talking to school staff, going to therapy, making and attending doctor's appointments, and doing online research. You likely feel exhausted and worn down. At times you may feel hopeless and worry that you might lose your temper and hurt him. When this happens, it is time to consider either a special day school or a boarding school.

We recognize that you should do what is best for your child and your family. If your son attends a special day school or boarding school, try not to worry about what grandma, cousin, or aunt so-and-so is going to say about your decision. They don't walk in your shoes or truly understand how stressful your daily life has become. Some parents cope with their son's stress by nail biting, smoking, drinking, or just keeping him in so many activities that he is away from them and the family. These actions may provide a temporary escape, but in the long run, they do not help him or you.

We recommend that when our clients choose a specialized day school for their son, they should look for one that offers these qualities:

◊ small classrooms with no more than 14 students (less is better);

◊ a teacher-to-student ratio of no more than 7 to 1;

◊ an environment with minimal distractions and unnecessary interruptions;

◊ a school philosophy of building upon strengths rather than just remediating deficits;

◊ an administrator who understands ADHD and provides teachers with ongoing professional development;

◊ teachers with specialized training in teaching and understanding boys with ADHD;

◊ teachers who know how to make accommodations and provide differentiated instruction;

◊ a daily schedule that places academics in the morning hours;

◊ a schedule that includes recess or physical activity every day; and

◊ a curriculum that teaches study skills and organizational strategies and utilizes multisensory and hands-on learning techniques.

Boarding Schools

Despite your best efforts and the effort of the school staff, your son may require an overwhelming amount of support that is all-consuming. Perhaps juvenile justice is involved, he's on a first-name basis with the sheriff, or you find yourself constantly expecting disaster. If he is out with friends and your phone rings, your heart skips a beat because you wonder if he is safe. Perhaps he continually and blatantly disobeys you and comes home way past his curfew. When this level of utter disobedience occurs, it may be time for him to attend a boarding school.

In fact, you may have threatened to send him to boarding school so many times you've lost count. In our experience, many parents issue that empty threat but few follow through. One mother said, "We constantly threaten to send my son to boarding school. We tell him that it's going to be his own choice because if he doesn't start making the right choices, he'll be going." This mom went on to say, "I don't know if I would ever have the nerve to do it, but it crosses my mind more than I'd like to think." Using boarding school as an empty threat is never helpful. Our advice to you is for you to rationally make the decision and then inform your son.

When you tell him about your decision, expect anger and shock. We find that often there are tears from both of you. Frame the discussion with your son in humility rather than anger or victory. Explain to him this is the "real deal" and he really is going. Remember that most boys with ADHD feel things before they can express them verbally, so expect him to be angry, cuss, kick or punch something, and shed tears. As one mom put it, "He was mad and upset, but then once he calmed down, he began to listen to us and accept what was happening." Give your son alone time if he needs it, but tell him you love him and that this is going help him change for the better. He may scream at you and say, "You don't love me or you wouldn't be doing this! You must hate me and I hate you too!" Explain that you can't accept any more empty promises from him to change, because you know he needs more assistance than he can get at home. Tell him that attending boarding school is short-term until he can learn to abide by your rules.

After telling him of your decision, you may consider involving him in the process of researching and making a final school selection. Ask him what he thinks of two different schools, both of which are acceptable to you. Show him the schools' websites and literature to teach him about what they offer. This can create buy-in and help your son believe he has some input and that his opinions are valued. He should definitely attend the campus visit with you.

One concern we hear from parents is that the boarding school will not know their son as well as they do. Most parents ask endless "what if" questions. What if he gets into a fight? What if his medications get mixed up? What if he doesn't go to the bathroom for weeks on end? What if he gets sick? What if he misses us so much that he cries himself to sleep? What if he feels abandoned? What if he hates us for doing this? To overcome this, you have to do your research, ask countless questions, make your choice, and then stay in contact with the administration and your son. Provide the emotional support that he needs.

We find it helpful to consider pros and cons when making any important decision. It's also important to teach your son how to make decisions based on pros and cons. Although any decision is always more than a simple count of pros vs. cons, it provides a starting point to help make your decision. Always consider the extraneous factors in your life and focus on the most important issues to your particular circumstances. Figure 9 includes our chart of boarding school pros and cons.

Once you've made the decision that boarding school is the right place for your son, the main question is, "How do we make the right boarding school choice when there are many to choose from?" This is a potentially life-changing decision, and it can be hard to know where to start. We find parents benefit when working with an educational consultant who specializes in boarding schools for boys with ADHD. This person can help provide support and guide you down the right path.

This is where we turn to our colleague, educational consultant Judi Robinovitz, for her boarding school advice. If you hire an educational consultant, be sure to choose one who uses a process similar to Judi's, which she explains here:

> We start by getting to know as much about a child and family as possible, assembling and evaluating a detailed history of the child's behavioral and academic history—from parents, from therapists and psychiatrists with whom the child has interacted,

Pros	Cons
Small class size	Expensive tuition
Increased individualized attention	May be isolating
Counseling services may be available	Emotionally difficult to separate from your son
Fresh start	Lack of appropriate role models
May increase his self-esteem	Cost of travel to and from home for holidays, weekends, etc.
Mentoring	Family separation
Highly structured, around-the-clock supervision	Requires adjustment to new environment

Figure 9. Boarding school pros and cons.

and from clinical and academic records. After identifying and discussing with parents the best placement options for their child, we present the resulting detailed profile to their admissions and clinical directors. We remain in the loop with parents and schools throughout the entire term of placement, monitoring a student's progress, advocating for the student, and ensuring that a student's and family's needs are being fully met. We even help a family plan the next steps after a therapeutic placement.

This is excellent advice because it emphasizes a team approach for helping your son. Again, you are not in this alone. If your son requires a boarding school, a good educational consultant can help point you in the right direction. If you decide to forgo working with an educational consultant, these are some of the questions you should ask when speaking with boarding school admissions directors. Make a chart with these questions on the left side and columns to the right where you can place each school's answers.

◊ How many counselors, psychologists, and/or psychiatrists are on staff at one time?

◊ What is the teacher-to-student ratio?

◊ How long does the average teacher stay employed with the school? Are they certified or licensed?

◊ How will my son be disciplined? What is the school's discipline plan?

◊ Is corporal punishment (e.g., spanking) or physical restraint used with students?

◊ Are parents encouraged to have their son take ADHD medication?

◊ What does a student's typical daily schedule look like?

◊ How frequently do parents get to talk and e-mail with their son?

◊ How long is your average student's stay?

◊ Is your school accredited, and will my son's coursework transfer to another school?

◊ What happens on weekends, long weekends, and holidays?

After you narrow your decision to the top two, visit each school's campus before making a final selection. The school may sound like the perfect fit when you talk with staff on the phone, read the catalogue, and study their website. Seeing the campus in person and talking to students will help finalize your decision.

Points to Consider

1. If your son's ADHD is impairing his school functioning significantly, he could meet the criteria for a 504 plan or Individualized Education Program (IEP).

2. Even though the disability perspective is difficult to accept, isn't it better for people to have an understanding of the neurobiological nature of his ADHD than to think he is just being difficult?

3. You are your son's most important advocate and always will be.

4. What specific struggles does your son have in his current classroom?

5. Are homeschooling or virtual school viable options for your son, and what resources exist in your community?

6. What benefits would there be in sending your son to a specialized day school or boarding school?

Action Steps to Take Now

1. Continue to educate yourself about your child's legal rights within the school system.

2. Think about your son's learning style, strengths, and weaknesses. What does he need in the classroom in order to do his best?

3. If he is struggling behaviorally or academically in the classroom with no support, contact the school about the necessity of a 504 plan or IDEA eligibility. Make sure you educate yourself so you can be a good advocate for him.

4. Develop a good working relationship with his teacher(s) and with other staff members who could assist him.

5. Be a positive and strong advocate for him.

Chapter 7

Pulling It All Together: The Dynamic Action Plan

Throughout this book we've given you action steps at the end of each chapter. Whether or not you've had the opportunity to apply them, our message to you is the same: Your son needs you, for you are his advocate, his champion, and a constant presence in his life. You realize that sitting idly does not help either of you, and by reading this book, you are working in the right direction. We created the Dynamic Action Plan as a reflective tool to help you prioritize your steps. As parents ourselves, we understand how it feels to become overwhelmed by your son's needs. You worry about what lies ahead. Despite his challenges, he is a unique person with a special purpose in life. You know there is hope for his future. You can help your son discover his purpose and grow in his journey.

The Dynamic Action Plan is a fluid and ever-changing document that you can complete and revisit as needed. We suggest you keep it in a visible location and review it monthly. The key is to begin by reflecting upon where you see your son 5 years from now, and if he's mature enough, to ask him to consider his next 5 years as well. Together, think about his future in the following ways:

◊ How old will he be?
◊ What will he physically look like?
◊ What will his personality be like?
◊ What do you expect from his behavior?
◊ How will he feel about himself?
◊ What will his ethics and character be like?
◊ Will he be able to make good decisions?
◊ What type of school will he attend?
◊ What interests and hobbies will he pursue?
◊ Who will his friends be?
◊ Will he have a job?
◊ Will he be taking medication?
◊ What strategies will he be using to manage his ADHD?
◊ What kind of support will he need at school? From his family?

We find that thinking about and predicting what your son will be doing in 5 years is an interesting exercise. For you it will stir various emotions, and you'll realize just how fast those years will pass. Now is the time to help him chart his course and lay the groundwork for skills that will help him in his life's journey.

After your time of reflection and discussion, select the areas that you feel should be the object of your focus, and put them in writing. Creating a written, permanent document is an important part of your Dynamic Action Plan's success. If it's not written down, you are less likely to refer back to your plan, and today's thoughts won't be as clearly defined. Also, your son will find many of these topics and responses encouraging, and we believe that making this Dynamic Action Plan a centerpiece in your life will provide tangible evidence of your commitment to his success. We prefer you to identify broad 5-year goals for your son and use intermediate steps to work back to today. Consider all aspects of his life—school, family, friends, leisure time and extracurricular activities, health and fitness, religious, etc.—as you complete these sentences:

◊   In 5 years, I/we see my son doing/being . . .

_____

_____

_____

_____

_____

◊   In 3 years, I/we see my son doing/being . . .

_____

_____

_____

_____

_____

◊   In one year, I/we see my son doing/being . . .

_____

_____

_____

_____

_____

In order for my son to achieve the vision I/we have for him at the 5-year mark, I need to do the following.

◊ Today:

_____

_____

_____

_____

◊ Tomorrow:

_____

_____

_____

_____

◊ Within one month:

_____

_____

_____

_____

◊ Within 6 months:

_____

_____

_____

_____

In order for my son to achieve the vision I/we have for him at the 5-year mark, he needs to do the following.

◊ Today:

_____

_____

_____

_____

◊ Tomorrow:

_____

_____

_____

_____

◊ Within one month:

_____

_____

_____

_____

◊ Within 6 months:

_____

_____

_____

_____

I/we believe my son's strengths include:

1. _____

   _____

   _____

   _____

2. _____

   _____

   _____

   _____

3. _____

   _____

   _____

   _____

4. _____

   _____

   _____

   _____

5. _____

   _____

   _____

   _____

I/we need to communicate these strengths to him as well as to the following people:

1. _____

   _____

   _____

   _____

2. _____

   _____

   _____

   _____

3. _____

   _____

   _____

   _____

4. _____

   _____

   _____

   _____

5. _____

   _____

   _____

   _____

Fill in this statement and share it with the people listed previously.

I/we can use his strength in _____

to help him _____.

In order for my son to achieve the vision I/we have for him at the 5-year mark, I/we need to obtain the support of the following individuals or professionals:

1. _____

_____

2. _____

_____

3. _____

_____

4. _____

_____

5. _____

_____

When I/we become discouraged or frustrated with his behavior or performance, I/we need to remember these things:

1. _____

_____

_____

_____

2. _____

_____

_____

_____

3. _____

_____

_____

_____

4. _____

_____

_____

_____

5. _____

_____

_____

_____

When I/we become discouraged or frustrated with his behavior or performance, I/we can count on these people for support:

1. _____

2. _____

3. _____

When my son becomes discouraged or frustrated with us or with his ADHD, he needs to remind himself of these things:

1. _____

_____

_____

_____

2. _____

_____

_____

_____

3. _____

_____

_____

_____

4. _____

_____

_____

_____

_____

5. _____

_____

_____

_____

When my son becomes discouraged or frustrated with us or with his ADHD, he can turn to the following people for support (other than myself):

1. _____

2. _____

3. _____

We'd like to close by thanking you for your effort and for the hard work you are doing on behalf of your son. In our experience as parents, we don't often hear many people say "Thank you" for how we are raising our boys with ADHD, but we know you deserve thanks. We understand your journey because we've traveled similar paths. Each day you work hard at raising your son, and one day he'll realize this. Helping your son make the most of his capabilities will be an accomplishment you can cherish all of your life. We can assure you that it will be worth every ounce of effort you put into it. Our compassion goes out to you.

References

Alderson, R. M., Rapport, M. D., Hudec, K. L., Sarver, D. E., & Kofler, M. J. (2010). Competing core processes in attention-deficit/hyperactivity disorder (ADHD): Do working memory deficiencies underlie behavioral inhibition deficits? *Journal of Abnormal Child Psychology, 38,* 497–507.

Alexander-Roberts, A. (2006). *AD/HD parenting handbook: Practical advice for parents from parents.* Lanham, MD: Rowman Littlefield.

American Academy of Pediatrics. (n.d.) *Connected kids: Safe, strong, secure.* Retrieved from http://www.aap.org/connectedkids/samples/tvviolence.htm

American Psychiatric Association. (2000). *Diagnostic and statistical manual of mental disorders* (4th ed., Text rev.). Washington, DC: Author.

Americans with Disabilities Act, 42 U.S.C. §§ 12102 et seq. (1990).

Armstrong, T. (1995) *The myth of the A.D.D. child.* New York, NY: Penguin.

Bailey, E. (2009). *ADHD in young children.* Retrieved from http://www.healthcentral.com/adhd/children-40947-5.html

Barkley, R. A. (1997). Behavioral inhibition, sustained attention, and executive functions: Constructing a unifying theory of ADHD. *Psychological Bulletin, 121,* 65–94.

Barkley, R. A. (2000a). *A new look at ADHD: Inhibition, time and self-control.* New York, NY: Guilford Press.

Barkley, R. A. (2000b). *Taking charge of ADHD. The complete, authoritative guide for parents.* New York, NY: Guilford Press.

Barkley, R. A. (2006). *Attention-Deficit Hyperactivity Disorder: A handbook for diagnosis and treatment* (3rd ed.). New York, NY: Guilford Press.

Barkley, R. A. (2007). School intervention for attention deficit hyperactivity disorder: Where to from here? *School Psychology Review, 36,* 279–286.

Barkley, R. A., & Cox, D. A. (2007). A review of driving risks and impairments associated with attention-deficit/ hyperactivity disorder and the effects of stimulant medication on driving performance. *Journal of Safety Research, 38,* 113–128.

Bower, B. (2006, October 28). Med-start kids: Pros, cons of Ritalin for preschool ADHD. *Science News, 170,* 12.

Breaden, M. (2007, September 12). Preschoolers with ADHD. *Education Week,* 5.

Centers for Disease Control and Prevention. (2011). *Attention Deficit Hyperactivity Disorder among children aged 5–17 years in the United States, 1998–2009.* Retrieved from http://www.cdc.gov/nchs/data/databriefs/db70.htm

Children and Adults With Attention Deficit/Hyperactivity Disorder. (2011). *Understanding ADHD: How is ADHD treated?* Retrieved from http://www.chadd.org/Content/CHADD/Understanding/Treatment/default.htm

Dahlin, K. I. E. (2011). Effects of working memory training on reading in children with special needs. *Reading and Writing, 24,* 479–491.

Dawson, M. M. (2007). The ideal versus the feasible when designing interventions for students with attention deficit hyperactivity disorder. *School Psychology Review, 36,* 274–278.

DuPaul, G. J. (2007). School-based interventions for students with attention deficit hyperactivity disorder: Current status and future directions. *School Psychology Review, 36,* 183–194.

Durheim, M., & Zeigler Dendy, C. A. (2006). Educational laws regarding students with AD/HD. In *CHADD educator's manual* (pp. 125–134). Landover, MD: CHADD.

Goldstein, S. (1999). Attention-deficit/hyperactivity disorder. In S. Goldstein & C. R. Reynolds (Eds.), *Handbook of neurodevelopmental and genetic disorders in children* (pp. 154–175). New York, NY: Guilford Press.

Goldstein, S. (2004). *What do we want from children with ADHD? Keeping a moving target in mind.* Retrieved from http://www.samgoldstein.com/cms/index.php/2004/09/what-do-we-want-from-children-with-adhd

Grady, M. M. (2010). The Multimodal Treatment Study of children with ADHD: Questions, answers, and controversies. *Psychopharmacology Educational Updates.* Retrieved from http://edb.pbclibrary.org:2077/ps/i.do?&id=GALE%7CA238349066&v=2.1&u=d0_mlpbcls&it=r&p=AONE&sw=w

Harvard Health Publications. (2007). *Preschool ADHD.* Retrieved from http://www.health.harvard.edu/press_releases/preschool-adhd

Holmes, J. H., Gathercole, S. E., Place, M., Dunning, D. L., Hilton, K. A., & Elliott, J. G. (2009). Working memory deficits can be overcome: Impacts of training and medication on working memory in children with ADHD. *Applied Cognitive Psychology, 24,* 827–836.

Individuals with Disabilities Education Improvement Act, Pub. Law 108-446 (December 3, 2004).

Katz, M. (2007, December). AD/HD safe driving program: A graduated license plan. *Attention*, 6–7.

Kofler, M. J., Rapport, M. D., Bolden, J., Sarver, D. E., & Raiker, J. S. (2010). ADHD and working memory: The impact of central executive deficits and exceeding storage/rehearsal capacity on observed inattentive behavior. *Journal of Abnormal Child Psychology, 38,* 149–161.

Koplewicz, H. S. (1996). *It's nobody's fault.* New York, NY: Random House.

Low, K. (2009, April 6). *ADHD in preschoolers—Signs of ADHD in preschoolers.* Retrieved from http://add.about.com/od/childrenandteens/a/preschool.htm

McConaughy, S., Volpe, R., Antshel, K., Gordon, M., & Eiraldi, R. (2011). Academic and social impairments of elementary school children with attention deficit hyperactivity disorder. *School Psychology Review, 40,* 200–225.

Mezzacappa, E., & Bucker, J. C. (2010). Working memory training for children with attention problems or hyperactivity: A school-based pilot study. *School Mental Health, 2,* 202–208.

Monastra, V. J. (2004). *Parenting children with ADHD: Lessons that medicine cannot teach.* Washington, DC: American Psychological Association.

Monastra, V. J., Lynn, S., Linden, M., Lubar, J. F., Gruzelier, J., & LaVaque, T. J. (2005). Electroencephalographic biofeedback in the treatment of attention-deficit/hyperactivity disorder. *Applied Psychophysiology and Biofeedback, 30,* 95–114.

Monastra, V. J., Monastra, D. M., & George, S. (2002). The effects of stimulant therapy, EEG biofeedback, and parenting style on the primary symptoms of attention-deficit/hyperactivity disorder. *Applied Psychophysiology and Biofeedback, 27,* 231–249.

National Dissemination Center for Children with Disabilities. (2010). *Attention-deficit/hyperactivity disorder.* Retrieved from http://nichcy.org/disability/specific/adhd

National Institute of Mental Health. (2009). *The Multimodal Treatment of Attention Deficit Hyperactivity Disorder study (MTA): Questions and answers.* Retrieved from http://www.nimh.nih.gov/trials/practial/mta

National Resource Center on ADHD. (2008). *Complementary and alternative treatments.* Retrieved from http://www.help4adhd.org/en/treatment/complementary/WWK6

NIH News. (2006). *Preschoolers with ADHD improve with low doses of medication.* Retrieved from http://www.nih.gov/news/pr/oct2006/nimh-16.htm

Parker, H. C. (2005). *Accommodations help students with attention deficit disorders* (ADAPT). Retrieved from http://www.addconsults.com/articles/full.php3?id=1353

Pelham, W. E., & Fabiano, G. A. (2008). Evidence-based psychosocial treatments for attention-deficit/hyperactivity disorder. *Journal of Clinical Child & Adolescent Psychology, 37,* 184–214.

Pharmacological and behavioral treatments for ADHD in preschoolers. (2009, April). *The Brown University Child and Adolescent Behavior Letter, 25*(4), 1–8.

Pliszka, S., & AACAP Work Group on Quality Issues. (2007). Practice parameter for the assessment and treatment of children and adolescents with attention-deficit/hyperactivity disorder. *Journal of American Academy of Child and Adolescent Psychiatry, 46,* 894–921.

Rapport, M. D., Bolden, J., Kofler, M. J., Sarver, D. E., Raiker, J. S., & Alderon, R. M. (2008). Hyperactivity in boys with attention-deficit/hyperactivity disorder (ADHD): A ubiquitous core symptom or manifestation of working memory deficits? *Journal of Abnormal Child Psychology, 37,* 521–534.

Ratey, N. A. (2008). *The disorganized mind.* New York, NY: St. Martin's Griffin.

Rief, S. F. (2008). *The ADD/ADHD checklist: A practical reference for parents and teachers* (2nd ed.).San Francisco, CA: Jossey-Bass.

Section 504 of the Rehabilitation Act, 29 U.S.C. Section 706 et. Seq. (1973).

Silver, L. B. (1999). *Dr. Larry Silver's Advice to Parents on ADHD.* New York, NY: Three Rivers Press.

Taylor, J. F. (2001). *Helping your ADD child.* Roseville, CA: Prima Publishing.

Teeter, P. A. (1998). *Interventions for ADHD: Treatment in developmental context.* New York, NY: Guilford Press.

Vitiello, B., & Sherrill, J. (2007). School-based interventions for students with attention deficit hyperactivity disorder: Research implications and prospects. *School Psychology Review, 36,* 287–290.

Weiss, G., & Hechtman, L. T. (1993). *Hyperactive children grow up.* New York, NY: Guilford Press.

Wendling, P. (2008, December 1). Full exam guides ADHD diagnosis in preschoolers. *Family Practice News,* 26.

Williams, N. I. (2010, September 30). Rare chromosomal deletions and duplications in attention-deficit hyperactivity disorder: A genome-wide analysis. *The Lancet, 376,* 1401–1408.

Wolraich, M. L. (2007, August). Preschoolers and AD/HD. *Attention,* 8–11.

Wright, P. (2009). *Four rules for raising children.* Retrieved from http://www.wrightslaw.com/nltr/09/nl.0106.htm#4

About the Authors

James W. Forgan and **Mary Anne Richey** have spent a combined 48 years working with boys with ADHD in school settings, in private practice, and at home. The first thing you need to know about the authors is that each of them is the parent of a happy, healthy son with ADHD.

James W. Forgan, Ph.D., is an Associate Professor and Licensed School Psychologist. He teaches others how to teach and assess children with ADHD and other types of learning disabilities at Florida Atlantic University in Jupiter, FL. In private practice, he works with families of children with ADHD and other learning differences. Jim consults with public and private schools doing workshops on ADHD, dyslexia, problem solving, and accommodations for learning disabilities.

Mary Anne Richey, M.Ed., also a Licensed School Psychologist, works for the school district of Palm Beach County and has a private practice. She also has experience as a middle school teacher, administrator, high school guidance counselor, and adjunct college instructor. Mary Anne has assisted many students with ADHD and their families over the years.

As a school psychologist, Jim always thought he had a solid grasp on the types of challenges his clients and families experienced. What an eye-opener it was when his son Teddy was diagnosed as a kindergartener. Now he really understands what it's like to walk the walk. He says the road has rough gravel, lots of bumps, and thankfully, some smooth patches along the way. Jim's sensitivity dramatically increased, and his advice is both practical and positive.

Mary Anne's experience was a little different. Her son was always very active but had excellent self-discipline and was strong academically. He didn't require an official diagnosis until his junior year of college, when he experienced difficulty staying focused long enough to finish engineering exams within a time limit. However, all along the way, he too required an understanding of his strengths and weaknesses and strategies to help him achieve success.

Throughout this book, Jim and Mary Anne help parents manage the issues they face and incorporate strategies to help their sons succeed in school and life. They share an integrated perspective on ADHD based on their experiences as parents and professionals, their academic research, and their interactions with so many other parents raising boys with ADHD.